M000032956

"In *Forty Days on Being a Two*, Hunter Mobley's wisdom, kindness, and hospitality flow from the pages. His insightful reflections are an invitation for Twos and *all* Enneagram types to nourish their souls. Savor the lessons, the stories, and the questions Hunter provides. They are a gift."

Drew Moser, author of *The Enneagram of Discernment* and cohost of *Fathoms: An Enneagram Podcast*

"Hunter Mobley is a relatable guide who creates a meaningful and nurturing experience with both integrity and his heart fully forward. Hunter not only stands in the trenches with us, he also lovingly rests on the shoulders of well-documented leaders and trailblazing teachers. In *Forty Days on Being a Two*, he has created a relatable plan that brilliantly gives words to feelings. I yelled, 'That's me too!' a dozen or more times. If you need that spark or nudge to launch out and fly in your most majestic jet stream, this is the perfect guide for a deeper dive into being an Enneagram Two. You will find new ways to grow alongside tangible strategy and spiritual guidance to rethink areas of your life where you once could not see past your own limitations. I walked away from this delightful journey rediscovering humility, grace, and love."

Rondal Richardson, community activist and entertainment philanthropist

"In this disarmingly honest and pastorally sensitive book, Hunter Mobley wisely guides Helpers like himself (Twos on the Enneagram) toward recognition of the downsides of their 'helpfulness.' He shows how, through fresh self-awareness and God's transformative love, they can find new, lifegiving, and appropriate ways to engage with their own needs and those of others."

Robert C. Spach, chaplain of Davidson College

"Hunter Mobley is a rising star in the Enneagram world. He combines his deep insight and experience as an Enneagram Two with a passion for helping others see how this ancient personality-typing system can lead to self-discovery and inner transformation. This is a must-read for anybody serious about spiritual growth, faith development, and relationship building."

Clay Stauffer, senior minister at Woodmont Christian Church, Nashville, Tennessee

"Gather 'round, my fellow Twos—this one's for you! In this devotional, Hunter Mobley paints a picture of the Enneagram working itself out through the life of a Two—the good (our front porch), the quirky (shower fights), and the ugly (an underdeveloped core self). This is an excellent forty-day journey that invites us all to turn inward and compassionately engage all parts of ourselves. As powerful as it is tender, this book is an incredible and dynamic guide for discovering our most authentic, healthy, and unhindered self."

Darin McKenna, pastor and Enneagram coach

"Journeying through these *Forty Days on Being a Two* with Hunter Mobley was like taking a pilgrimage with a trusted companion who knows me and sees into the deepest places of my soul where light and dark both reside. He travels with readers on this journey in an honest and genuine manner, not shying away from his own transparency and holding our hands as together we embrace vulnerability. I will use the reflection questions and prayers again. I am grateful to Hunter for sharing his gift of teaching in his relatable style that not only highlights his depth of knowledge of the Enneagram but also his heartfelt passion to set a place at the table for everyone."

Mary Jane Cole, spiritual director, Sacred Path

"To be understood is perhaps one of the most satisfying experiences of life! And that was my sensation as I read *Forty Days on Being a Two* by Hunter Mobley. Each day's reflection shed light into me from a new angle. Some rays exposed the shadow side of my Two-ness, while others illuminated my genius. The invitation of this series and this book is a to cast a steady gaze into what makes and motivates us, to reflect and pray into what we discover, so that little by little we grow into our most authentic selves and increase our capacity for love. A worthy endeavor!"

Beth A. Booram, codirector of Fall Creek Abbey and author of *When Faith Becomes Sight* with her husband, David

HUNTER MOBLEY

SUZANNE STABILE, SERIES EDITOR

FORTY DAYS ON
BEING A TWO

 ENNEAGRAM DAILY REFLECTIONS

ivp

An imprint of InterVarsity Press
Downers Grove, Illinois

InterVarsity Press
P.O. Box 1400, Downers Grove, IL 60515-1426
ivpress.com
email@ivpress.com

©2020 by Hunter Russell Mobley

*All rights reserved. No part of this book may be reproduced in any form without
written permission from InterVarsity Press.*

*InterVarsity Press® is the book-publishing division of InterVarsity Christian
Fellowship/USA®, a movement of students and faculty active on campus at
hundreds of universities, colleges, and schools of nursing in the United States of
America, and a member movement of the International Fellowship of Evangelical
Students. For information about local and regional activities, visit intervarsity.org.*

*All Scripture quotations, unless otherwise indicated, are taken from The Holy Bible,
New International Version®, NIV®. Copyright © 1973, 1978, 1984, 2011 by
Biblica, Inc.™ Used by permission of Zondervan. All rights reserved worldwide.
www.zondervan.com. The "NIV" and "New International Version" are trademarks
registered in the United States Patent and Trademark Office by Biblica, Inc.™*

*While any stories in this book are true, some names and identifying information
may have been changed to protect the privacy of individuals.*

Enneagram figure by InterVarsity Press

Cover design and image composite: David Fassett
Interior design: Daniel van Loon
*Images: gold foil background: © Katsumi Murouchi / Moment Collection /
        Getty Images*
*   paper texture background: © Matthieu Tuffet / iStock / Getty Images Plus*

ISBN 978-0-8308-4744-0 (print)
ISBN 978-0-8308-4745-7 (digital)

Printed in the United States of America ∞

*InterVarsity Press is committed to ecological stewardship and to the conservation
of natural resources in all our operations. This book was printed using sustainably
sourced paper.*

Library of Congress Cataloging-in-Publication Data
A catalog record for this book is available from the Library of Congress.

P 20 19 18 17 16 15 14 13 12 11 10 9 8 7 6 5 4 3 2 1
Y 37 36 35 34 33 32 31 30 29 28 27 26 25 24 23 22 21 20

WELCOME TO
ENNEAGRAM DAILY REFLECTIONS

Suzanne Stabile

T he Enneagram is about nine ways of seeing. The reflections in this series are written from each of those nine ways of seeing. You have a rare opportunity, while reading and thinking about the experiences shared by each author, to expand your understanding of how they see themselves and how they experience others.

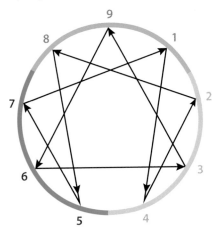

I've committed to teaching the Enneagram, in part, because I believe every person wants at least these two things: to belong, and to live a life that has meaning. And I'm sure that learning and working with the Enneagram has the potential to help all of us with both.

Belonging is complicated. We all want it, but few of us really understand it. The Enneagram identifies—with more accuracy than any other wisdom tool I know—why we can achieve belonging more easily with some people than with others. And it teaches us to find our place in situations and groups without having to displace someone else. (I'm actually convinced that it's the answer to world peace, but some have suggested that I could be exaggerating just a bit.)

If our lives are to have meaning beyond ourselves, we will have to develop the capacity to understand, value, and respect people who see the world differently than we do. We will have to learn to name our own gifts and identify our weaknesses, and the Enneagram reveals both at the same time.

The idea that we are all pretty much alike is shattered by the end of an introductory Enneagram workshop or after reading the last page of a good primer. But for those who are teachable and open to receiving Enneagram wisdom about each of the nine personality types, the shock is accompanied by a beautiful and unexpected gift: they find that they have more compassion for themselves and more grace for others, and it's a guarantee.

The authors in this series, representing the nine Enneagram types, have used that compassion to move toward a greater understanding of themselves and others whose lives intersect with theirs in big and small ways. They write from experiences that reflect racial and cultural difference, and they have been influenced by different faith beliefs. In working with spiritual directors, therapists, and pastors, they identified many of their own habits and fears, behaviors and motivations, gifts and challenges. And they courageously talked with those who are close to them about how they are seen and experienced in relationship.

As you begin reading, I think it will be helpful for you to be generous with yourself. Reflect on your own life—where you've been and where you're going. And I hope you will consider the difference between change and transformation. *Change* is when we take on something new. *Transformation* occurs when something old falls away, usually beyond our control. When we see a movie, read a book, or perhaps hear a sermon that we believe "changed our lives," it will seldom, if ever, become transformative. It's a good thing and we may have learned a valuable life lesson, but that's not transformation. Transformation occurs when you have an experience that changes the way you understand life and its mysteries.

When my Dad died, I immediately looked for the leather journal I had given to him years before with the request that he fill it with stories and things he wanted me to know. He had only written on one page:

*Anything I have achieved or accomplished
in my life is because of the gift of your mother
as my wife. You should get to know her.*

I thought I knew her, but I followed his advice, and it was one of the most transformative experiences of my life.

From a place of vulnerability and generosity, each author in this series invites us to walk with them for forty days on their journeys toward transformation. I hope you will not limit your reading to only your number. Read about your spouse or a friend. Consider reading about the type you suspect represents your parents or your siblings. You might even want to read about someone you have little affection for but are willing to try to understand.

You can never change *how* you see, but you can change what you *do* with how you see.

ON BEING A TWO

I n 2014, life gave me an offering: I was seated next to
Suzanne and Joe Stabile at a dinner party. A true *happy-
stance*, not just happenstance. We were all participating in
a weekend gathering at The Gasparilla Inn in Boca Grande,
Florida, as part of Telemachus, an intergenerational
Christian networking community. Suzanne was leading a
pre-conference day on the Enneagram, which I did not
attend. I had never heard of the Enneagram. And if I had
heard of it from anyone other than this charming, grand-
motherly lady with the drawl of Floydada, Texas, on her
lips, I'm sure that I would have thought that the word
sounded too near to a Pentagram.

Suzanne won me over before our chicken and potatoes
were served. We became instant friends and, as luck would
have it, she was traveling two weeks later to my hometown
of Nashville to lead a day-long "Know Your Number"
workshop—her signature Enneagram introduction—for the
staff at Otter Creek Church of Christ. I snuck in, listening
with eyes wide and heart open, as she shared eight hours of

wisdom about the nine Enneagram types. I discovered that I am a Two, like her. And from that day on, I have been Suzanne's student and she, my teacher.

Suzanne delivered the Enneagram to me in much the same way that Father Richard Rohr delivered it to her thirty years earlier: as a passing down of wisdom from apprentice to student. My story has been forever changed by Suzanne and by the Enneagram. She and it have been my companions through some of the most formative times in my life so far as a thirty-five-year-old pastor, lawyer, and teacher.

The Enneagram does not exist in a vacuum. It invites you into conversations and awakenings that are theological, relational, and personal. This is why the Enneagram, historically, was rarely taught without a companion faith tradition. In this devotional, I layer the wisdom of the Christian story with the wisdom of the Enneagram. The Enneagram not only describes personality but leads us to discover mysterious places in ourselves that lie beyond personality—namely our souls, or the Christ in you and the Christ in me.

And what a mystery is a soul!

I'm embarrassed to say that after years of serving as a pastor, I still don't have any clear understanding of what a soul is beyond the place in our consciousness that flutters at the sight of truth, beauty, and goodness. A soul is not something that we search for and capture. It is something that we learn to recognize and observe with awe and reverence. The Enneagram helps us to declutter the bulk from our personalities so that our souls can reveal themselves to us.

The past five years have been good years for the Enneagram. If you have paid attention recently to Instagram or pop Christianity, it is likely that you have bumped up against this old tool in its new moment. And because everything contains its opposite, recent exposure for the Enneagram is both blessing and curse. The blessing has been open doors and open ears for its wisdom. The curse has been the reduction of what traditionally was received as slowly applied wisdom to soundbites and numbered lists. For nearly all of its history, the Enneagram has been delivered in narrative form from teacher to student, either through retreat or through reading long-form descriptions of all nine types. If you learned your Enneagram type through a test, my invitation is to hold that loosely and take some time to read a long-form book about the Enneagram or attend a workshop taught by a master teacher.

As a Tennessean, I was born to love one of the hallmarks of good southern architecture: a gracious front porch. And if you're like me—having spent much of my adult life with stoops and condo welcome mats—you may have pictured a future life with a porch swing, ferns, and fall pumpkins. When I think about how to make sense of the Enneagram as a personality tool, I use the metaphor of a house, with the front porch and living room as personality and the rooms beyond as deeper, soul-ish spots.

In a house, the front porch and living room are the spaces typically most ready to receive guests. We curate these spaces in ways that reflect our values. We turn the porch lights on (or off!) as a way of telling people when we're open for their visit. When we sweep and straighten and clean, it's these spaces that get our first attention. We justify a bit of mess in other rooms because the Halloween trick-or-treater won't be going past the front porch and living room.

In my childhood home, our living room had white carpet, which is something that would have never survived in the den, kitchen, or bedrooms. Our living room could have white carpet because it was reserved for company, not for intimate family gatherings. Christmas mornings and Kentucky basketball viewing parties all happened in rooms that were farther back in the house.

The Enneagram describes nine different front porches and living rooms—nine different ways that the world first meets us. And whether swept up or messed up, our personalities are the most curated parts of ourselves. We've worked on them through the years with intention. Just like our homes' front porches and living rooms, our personalities are the recognizable parts of our beings.

But our homes have depths beyond front porches and living rooms, and so do we. You may encounter kitchens, dens, family rooms, bedrooms, and back porches. And the really good stuff happens in these rooms. Around the kitchen table is where we have our late-night intimate conversations. The den is where our closest family huddles up on the couch to watch Netflix. The bedroom is where we allow someone, under low light, to see us in our most unguarded state. Kitchens, dens, family rooms, and bedrooms all represent the places in us that are beyond personality. They represent our souls. They represent our essences. They represent the Christ in you and the Christ in me.

As Twos, our front porches and living rooms look like helpful, attentive, and emotionally intelligent responders. We have well-curated our reputations as people who can be counted on. We're the people of "yes!" But, beyond our front porches and living rooms are a diversity of unexpressed and unmet feelings and needs. Tiredness, loneliness, grief, disappointment, and longing live beside joy, gratitude, and hope in our kitchens, dens, and bedrooms.

This devotional is designed to explore the shadow and light of our front porches and living rooms as Twos so that we can find our way beyond them into the deeper places of our souls. Let's begin today considering what our personalities look like to the outside world. And let's begin using this self-knowledge to help us begin our journeys toward our healthiest selves.

If you aren't a Two, you are welcome too! You are invited through this journey to discover more about the unspoken wounds, motivations, and longings of your friends and family members who are Twos, the best number on the

Enneagram—Jesus' number! *Just kidding!* But, seriously, because the Enneagram invites us all into a story that is larger than our own individual stories, it is my hope that we will all take the time to understand as much as we can about all nine Enneagram types as we grow in compassion for ourselves and for others. Thank you for being our Two ally—we're grateful!

◎ ◎ ◎ ◎

A forty-day journey carries particular significance in the Christian story. Jesus spent forty days fasting in the desert before his public ministry began. The Gospels detail the forty days that spanned Jesus' resurrection and ascension. In Genesis's flood narrative, the rain fell for forty days. For centuries, Christians have spent forty days during Lent to reflect and purify themselves for the celebration of Easter. A lot can happen in forty days!

As you embark on your own forty-day journey, my prayer is that this devotional invites you to discover new things about yourself, leads you into more self-compassion as you realize that you are not alone, and promotes transformation as we discover together how to live into ways of being a Two that are healthy for each of us. Each day ends with reflection questions or a suggested prayer or practice. Use these as you wish, or not at all. The important thing is to follow your own inner lights—the lights of the Spirit stirring in you.

May the God who balances all things—light and dark, body and soul, spirit and truth, suffering and joy—work a thousand tiny miracles in all of us to call us back to our truest wholeness, beyond personality, where deep cries out to deep.

Let the journey begin!

LET IT GO

AS TWOS, we are natural-born helpers and natural-born fixers. People are drawn to us, and we are drawn to them. In a task-oriented culture, Twos have an important role to play in connecting with people. But all of that helping can come at a cost.

We have old patterns of over-saving, over-fixing, and over-rescuing that need to fall away. Old lies that tell you that self-disclosure will lead to people leaving you need to fall away. Old messages that tell you that it isn't okay to express your own needs and feelings need to fall away.

We're masters at gritting our teeth and ignoring our own pain and swirling feelings. We intuitively come to Enneagram work hoping to discover what steps we can take to help ourselves and fix our problems. But what we really need is transformation, not change. We need to open up, allow ourselves to be seen, and let go of old things so that there is room for God's new.

Change is good; change helps us. The spiritual life involves change too. Our spiritual journeys invite us all to change our behaviors at different points in our lives.

Transformation, however, is less about taking new things on and more about letting old things fall away. We can work our way to change, but we need to open up our hands to transformation. Any transformative work that God has done in me has been God's work, not my own, and it has happened as I let go and allowed God, in mystery, to work inside of me.

The Enneagram is a tool about transformation, not change. The Enneagram invites us to embrace the best and the worst of us. It invites us into non-judgmental self-awareness and compassion. It invites us to discover how our wounds might become, through God's help, sacred wounds.

Let us continue to allow the wisdom of the Enneagram to lead us toward the transformation that comes as old patterns of thinking, feeling, and doing fall away, allowing new growth to bloom. "And we all . . . are being transformed into his image with ever-increasing glory, which comes from the Lord, who is the Spirit" (2 Corinthians 3:18).

How do people first experience you?

Do people's first impressions fit what you know to be true of your inner self?

WOUNDED HEALERS

WHEN I AM ASKED to give a brief explanation of the nine Enneagram types, I focus on the wounds that define each number. The thing that I love the most about the Enneagram is that it doesn't identify personalities based on behaviors—it focuses on our core motivations, which are formed through wounds that we first experience in childhood.

As Twos, our wounds teach us to minimize our own needs and feelings. They teach us to over-identify with the needs and feelings of everyone around us. Our wounds teach us to find love and belonging through being helpful and attentive, and not demanding too much for ourselves.

I picked up these wounds so early that I can't identify all of the places that they emerged from. As a child, I felt like I needed to be "fine" and use all of my energy to help the people around me. I still hesitate to name my own feelings and needs. My strongest defense tactic is asking people endless questions about themselves. If I can fill a lunchtime appointment with conversation about the other person, I can avoid disclosing much at all about myself. I can't tell you how many meals and meetups have ended with the other person saying, "Gosh, we didn't have any time to talk about everything going on with you—let's make sure we do that next time!"

Our wounds motivate our feelings and actions. My wounds as a Two are what lead me to over-identify with the feelings of the people around me and to over-meddle in friends' lives.

Our invitation is to discover how our wounds can become sacred wounds. Richard Rohr writes, "All healthy religion shows you what to do with your pain. If we do not transform our pain, we will most assuredly transmit it. . . . If we cannot find a way to make our wounds into sacred wounds, we invariably become negative or bitter."

The wounds that have caused us as Twos to spend our lifetimes minimizing our own needs and feelings can become our sacred wounds. Our wounds can be redeemed. Our wounds can lead to our healing.

Can you find God in your wounds?

God, who heals broken things and shines light into every darkness, into our wounds, come. Amen.

NAKED AND NOT ASHAMED

MY HOME IN THE AMERICAN SOUTH has a history full of glory and horror. One of the songs that haunts our history of racism is the unofficial Confederate anthem, "Dixie," that includes the lyrics "look away, look away, look away Dixie Land." In the South, these lyrics remind me of our tendency to gloss over our history of trails of tears and Jim Crow with sweet tea and polite manners.

As an Enneagram Two, these lyrics challenge me to recognize how much my shame has caused me, through under-recognition of my own feelings and needs, to say "look away, look away, look away." Only in my midthirties have I started to become comfortable uncovering my feelings as I hear God's voice calling me from hiding to step into the light of truth.

According to the Genesis narrative, after Adam and Eve ate the fruit from the tree of the knowledge of good and evil, they became aware of their nakedness and hid from God. God came searching for them and made them clothes to cover their newly awakened bodies. Shame was introduced into the story, and from Genesis until now, the human experience has been one of hiding from self, from others, and from God.

Twos are well acquainted with shame. It is our intuitive core emotion. Often before our other emotions such as anger, sadness, and disappointment get expressed, they are translated and misidentified as shame. Like Adam and Eve in Genesis, shame causes us to hide. We hide our true needs and our honest feelings. Shame tells us that our needs and feelings are less important than the needs and feelings of other people. Shame tells us that no one really wants to understand our needs and feelings. And shame tells us that people will leave us or disappoint us if we express our deepest selves.

In response to the Two's wounding message, or the "unconscious" childhood message as described by Enneagram authority Don Riso, that we shouldn't have too many needs of our own, we hide from ourselves, from others, and from God through busy over-attending to the needs of people around us. We hope that our busyness will distract us and others (and maybe even God!) from any inquiry into who we truly are and what we truly need.

But God comes for us and calls us out of hiding and into the light. God doesn't shame us for our shame. God will even make some clothes for us to cover up if that's what it takes to draw us from our self-imposed isolation. God invites us to step out, in all of our ugliness and beauty, to give the world the best gift that we can give: an honest, open, actualized self.

In Genesis 3:9, God calls to Adam and Eve (and to you), "Where are you?" How has shame sent you into hiding?

What parts of your true self have you kept hidden out of shame?

PRIDE COMES BEFORE THE FALL

ENNEAGRAM WISDOM names a core passion associated with each number. Christian students of the Enneagram will recognize that the nine passions correspond with Evagirus Ponticus's seven deadly sins, plus two—fear and deceit. Traditional Enneagram schools—influenced by Oscar Ichazo—have used the language of passions to describe the anger, pride, deceit, envy, avarice, fear, gluttony, lust, and sloth that characterize the nine Enneagram types, but some modern schools, particularly those aligned with Jesuit or evangelical iterations of the Enneagram, have reframed the passions as sins. Regardless of the language that we use, each Enneagram number's passion leads to alienation from self, others, and God.

The passion for Twos is pride. When I first learned this piece of Enneagram wisdom, I had to learn the Enneagram definition for pride. As Twos, we don't often exhibit pride in the usual things that people associate with prideful people. We don't boast in our bank accounts, our houses, our promotions, or our cars. At my first "Know Your Number" seminar, as I was initially learning about my Two-ness, I felt like I had pretty much mastered the sin of pride since I didn't try to draw attention to my accomplishments. But, then I learned what pride for Twos really means.

Twos are not prideful in traditional ways that we associate with American accomplishment and greed. Pride for me as a Two looks like this: *Hey there! How are you doing? Oh, you're not doing so hot? Well, here's the good news: I'm doing fine, which means that I have all of the energy and attention that most people direct toward their own needs to direct toward your needs!*

Our pride causes us to underacknowledge our own neediness and see ourselves as fixers for other people, when the truth is that we are the ones needing help. We are prideful in not affirming our own feelings and needs. We unknowingly place ourselves on the pedestal of pride as we put on everyone else's oxygen masks while we fail to realize that the person most in need of oxygen is us!

I am learning to be honest about the pride that keeps me in the unhealthiest behaviors of my personality. When I do things that aren't mine to do and help people who haven't asked for my help, it's a sure sign that pride has taken over the day.

Do you connect with the passion of pride?

How do you recognize pride showing up in
your personality?

God of truth, into our underacknowledgement, come.
Amen.

AND THE GREATEST
OF THESE IS LOVE

AS ENNEAGRAM TWOS, we have a special and complicated relationship with love. It's easy and intuitive for us to love other people, but it's challenging for us to love ourselves.

Self-love is hard for all of the Enneagram numbers, namely Twos, Threes, and Fours, that have shame as their core emotion. We don't always believe that we are worthy of the love that we shower on other people. We are not always sure that we will be loved, so we settle for being wanted and needed. We aren't sure that we are lovable if we're not helpful or valuable.

If you have been to a wedding, I'm guessing that you have heard 1 Corinthians 13. In my fourth grade Bible drill, I learned that 1 Corinthians 13 is commonly known as the love chapter. It's one of the beautiful poems of the Bible. We recall, "Love is patient, love is kind." However, if you spend time studying the gifts of the Holy Spirit that Paul describes in 1 Corinthians 12 and 14, you will discover that 1 Corinthians 13 happens right in the middle of Paul's instructions about prophecy.

If I have the gift of prophecy and can fathom all mysteries and all knowledge, and if I have a faith that can move mountains, but do not have love, I am nothing. If I give all I possess to the poor and give over my body to hardship that I may boast, but do not have love, I gain nothing.

Love is patient, love is kind. It does not envy, it does not boast, it is not proud. It does not dishonor others, it is not self-seeking, it is not easily angered, it keeps no record of wrongs. Love does not delight in evil but rejoices with the truth. It always protects, always trusts, always hopes, always perseveres.

Love never fails. But where there are prophecies, they will cease; where there are tongues, they will be stilled; where there is knowledge, it will pass away. (1 Corinthians 13:2-8)

Why does Paul break up his set of specific instructions on the use of spiritual gifts to insert a poem about love? After spending some time in these passages, my feeling is that Paul knew that it was important to remind us—in the middle of a sermon about gifts—that the fruit of the Spirit, particularly the fruit of love, is more important than the gifts. It's almost as if Paul knew that we would fight over the gifts. We would worry about who had them and who didn't. We would worry about how they can be used and when they should be stopped. Paul needed to remind us that there is a greater thing than the gifts.

After all of the prophecies have ended and all of the tongues have stopped; after everything is said and done; and, as Andrew Peterson wrote in his beautiful song, "after the last tear falls," there are three things that remain: faith, hope, and love. And the greatest of these is love. Ultimately, what matters is not whether we practiced any of the gifts—what matters is whether we were open to giving and receiving love.

Today, hear Paul's letter of love from 1 Corinthians 13 as something that you are worthy of. Feel the love that you give to the rest of the world coming back toward you today. Loving others is our gift as Twos, but loving ourselves is our invitation.

Love never ends.

You are worthy of love because you belong to the universe and to God, not because you are helpful and attentive to other people.

God of love, help me to find my place in your ever-present, always abundant love. Amen.

WHO AM I?

MY SENSE IS THAT all humans are looking for two things: love and belonging. We discover and embrace love and belonging in unique and different ways, but we are all on a similar quest to find our paths toward these two existential ideals. Brené Brown, the brilliant researcher and storyteller, says that parents have only one job—to instill the message into their children that they are imperfect and wired for struggle, but are worthy of love and belonging.

The problem for Enneagram Twos is that we often truncate our truest selves to find love and belonging. I get people to like me by being less like me. As Twos who over-identify with the dreams and desires of people around us, our core selves are underdeveloped.

When I was in my early twenties and discovering what I wanted to be when I grew up, I noticed an internal pattern. If I listened extensively to someone describe their passion and work, I began to develop a passion for the same thing. Every career talk sponsored by the career services department made me wonder if I should change course and move in the direction of the speaker.

One of the defining moments that illustrates this problem is when I went to a lunch during my second year of law school that was sponsored by the FBI. Two FBI agents brought boxes of pepperoni pizza and engaging stories about the exciting and ever-changing career of an FBI agent. I went home that night and thought to myself, *I think I want to be an FBI agent!* Fortunately, this thought was so far from all of the interests that I have had over my lifetime that I was able to stop and laugh at myself. I am terrified of guns, and I don't keep secrets well. Even if I applied to the FBI, they wouldn't take me!

I began to realize how many times I shift my dreams, passions, and goals to match those of other people. I have spent a lifetime finding love and belonging through identifying the needs and interests of people around me and re-ordering mine to fit. I have spent a good portion of my life out of touch with my own feelings, needs, and passions. My core self is underdeveloped.

What would our lives look like if we stopped trying to get people to like us by being less like us, and could just be ourselves?

You are worthy of love and belonging just because you are you! Repeat this phrase to yourself today.

DIVIDED NO MORE

INTEGRITY DOESN'T ALWAYS coincide with good behavior. My favorite architect, Frank Lloyd Wright, was a man of integrity. His life and work represent an adherence to standards and principles that he never wavered from. Yet, his personal life was less than the Christian ideal.

When we think of people of integrity, we think of Bible figures such as Daniel, who was committed to his beliefs even in the face of what seemed like certain death by hungry lions. The book that bears his name in the Old Testament depicts a man who was the same person in public that he was behind closed doors. His lifestyle and choices represent someone who, in a classic understanding of the word *integrity*, was whole and not divided.

Integrity is less about whether we are a person who makes morally virtuous choices and more about becoming a person who is undivided. We are divided when we act in ways that are untrue to the person we know ourselves to be. This is why both Frank Lloyd Wright and Daniel can be held up as men of integrity—both followed their own North Star in public and in private, seven days a week.

As Twos, we shift our shapes to fit with people whose love and admiration we want. Traditionally, Threes are described as the chameleons of the Enneagram, but Twos adapt as well—we just adapt for different reasons. Enneagram Threes adapt and shapeshift their decisions, actions, and goals to meet their current environment's standard of success. Enneagram Twos adapt and shapeshift their feelings, beliefs, and actions to match those of people around them. This is why I can honestly say that many times I become less like me in order to get people to like me.

As is the case with Enneagram Threes, our shapeshifting as Twos is intuitive and not meant to deceive. We are so good at empathizing with the feelings and beliefs of other people that we pick them up as our own in order to make connections.

Parker Palmer, who self-identifies as an Enneagram Three, wrote about vocation in his book *Let Your Life Speak*: "The people who plant the seeds of movements make a critical decision: they decide to live 'divided no more.' *They decide no longer to act on the outside in a way that contradicts some truth about themselves that they hold deeply on the inside. . . .* 'I will no longer act as if I were less than the whole person I know myself inwardly to be.'"

Do we have the courage to become people of integrity by deciding to live divided no more?

How have you contradicted the truth about yourself in order to make connections with other people?

WHITHER THOU GOEST I WILL GO

THE STORY OF RUTH is one of my favorite stories in the Bible. Ruth was living with her family in her native region of Moab when tragedy struck: her husband, father-in-law, and brother-in-law died. The only people left were her mother-in-law, Naomi, and her sister-in-law, Orpah. The tradition of the time dictated that Ruth and Orpah were to return to their families of origin to find new husbands, and that Naomi was to return to her hometown of Bethlehem to live out the rest of her days as a widow dependent on charity from her community.

Ruth broke tradition and pledged to care for her mother-in-law, Naomi. She committed to leaving her home in Moab and journeying with Naomi into the foreign territory of Bethlehem, where Ruth would be a foreigner for the rest of her life. In the oft-quoted passage, she tells Naomi, "Wherever you go, I will go; wherever you live, I will live. Your people will be my people, and your God will be my God" (Ruth 1:16 NLT).

The story of Ruth and Naomi's love for one another is one of the most beautiful in the Bible. Ruth's sacrifice represents the best ideals of love, friendship, and commitment.

Ruth's story also represents an opportunity for reflection for Enneagram Twos. As Twos, we identify intuitively with Ruth's choice to abandon the conventions of the day to remain in relationship with someone that she loved. In one of C. S. Lewis' letters, he wrote, "If I had to give a piece of advice to a young man about a place to live, I think I should say, 'sacrifice almost everything to live where you can be near your friends.'" Lewis' advice resonates with us as Twos.

According to the Bible and the way that the story unfolded, Ruth was right to throw caution to the wind and abandon tradition to pursue relationship with someone that she loved. The invitation in Ruth's story for Twos is to ask ourselves this question: When we, like Ruth, make great sacrifices to be in relationship with someone else, is it born from a true desire to build a mutual friendship, or is it born from a need to become someone's rescuer so that we can be the heroes who save the day? This is such a hard thing to truly determine. It takes a lot of thinking, time, and honesty to figure out if our relational pursuits are mutual and healthy. Sometimes, as Twos, we make sacrifices more from a need to be needed than from a desire for true and honest connection.

Many of the times when I have put my own needs on hold to care for someone else, it has been because I wanted to be seen as the person who can always be counted on to step in to save the day. Ultimately, when I act from this motivation, it ends up hurting me and the other person.

As Twos, we are invited to read Ruth's story and gather the beautiful things that it can teach us about commitment and sacrifice; but we are also invited, by Ruth's story, to recognize our propensity to sit in the seat of the rescuer. We, like Ruth, will need wisdom and help from God to know when our motivation to help at great sacrifice is healthy and when it is unhealthy.

Our spiritual journeys also invite us to add in new practices—some of which are very difficult at first, but we know that they will pay off in the long run. The spiritual practice of centering prayer is one that can help Twos learn to sit at the feet of God. This is a meditation practice that simply involves closing your eyes and letting go of your thoughts so that you can become totally open to the unseen work of God inside of you. Begin with twenty minutes—or even five minutes—of simply sitting with God.

MESSIAH-MAKING

WHEN I WAS FIRST LEARNING about the nine personality types that make up the Enneagram, I had a hard time deciding whether I was a Two or a Nine. There are a lot of common characteristics between Twos and Nines. Both numbers are go-along-get-along types. Both Twos and Nines sacrifice their own hopes, desires, and needs and align themselves with the hopes, desires, and needs of other people.

The distinguishing factor that finally led me to discover that I was a Two and not a Nine was the distinction between merging and adapting. Nines merge, and Twos adapt.

Merging occurs when Nines align their interests with the interests of someone else. When Nines merge, they lose touch with their own interests and recalibrate to happily share the interests of the person they merged with. Adapting occurs when Twos recognize that someone has an interest other than their own, and they push down their own interest to connect with the other person.

The problem with adapting for us Twos is that adapting may also involve martyring. When we adapt, we don't forget our own interests or preferences. We take pride in our self-sacrifice and expect to be rewarded for giving some part of ourselves up. If the other person doesn't respond to our adapting with gratitude or appreciation, we can become frustrated and resentful.

The cure for our martyrdom as Twos is to recognize how quickly we have a tendency to adapt our needs, preferences, and desires to those of someone else, and to stop! In the moment, we think that adapting is the path to deeper connection, but in reality, it plants a seed of resentment in our hearts that ultimately can be poison in the relationship.

When I find myself feeling unappreciated and undervalued by someone, I can almost always find a corresponding time that I gave up part of myself to adapt to that person's needs, preferences, or desires.

There is a Messiah and I'm not him! This is a mantra that I have learned to apply to my life as a Two who takes (too much) pride in being needed and necessary. It sounds exaggerated, but as Twos there is truth in the idea that we think of ourselves as little messiahs to our families and friends.

One problem, among many, with messiah-making is that we also make martyrs of ourselves. We hang ourselves on crosses of our own making and hope that the world will pass by and see how much we have given and how greatly we have sacrificed. When I do this, I can almost hear people thinking, *Get off the cross; we need the nails!*

I am learning to find a consistent identity that is not tied to whomever or wherever I am serving. I can save myself and everyone else from my martyring if I never make myself someone's messiah in the first place. The person who needs saving, fixing, and rescuing the most is me! And I am learning to devote more attention to letting Jesus be Messiah for me and for the world.

Where is resentment showing up in your heart as a result from adapting?

God, into my resentments and hiding, come. Help me to free myself and others by being honest about my true needs. Amen.

AT THE CENTER

AS TWOS, we are often the centerpieces of our families and communities. We like to be in the middle of things, we like to be involved, we like to volunteer, we like to be needed, and we like to be conscientious and helpful. It's no wonder that when we are healthy, our family members talk about us as glue players and people who can always be counted on.

If I'm being honest, I take a lot of pride in being a centerpiece of different communities that I am a part of. I want to be at the center of things, drawing people in, and helping everyone stay connected. Like the hub of a wheel, I want all the spokes to point to me.

The question, however, is: Am I a centerpiece in a way that blesses everyone in the community to belong and be free, or am I a centerpiece in a manipulative way that requires people's place in the community to be dependent on me?

I enjoy introducing friends to each other. A couple of years ago, I introduced two friends who I thought would have a lot in common. It turns out that they did. These two friends quickly developed a friendship of their own that included meals, text messages, and trips together with their families. In the early days, I felt happy that I was able to broker a connection between two people that obviously shared a lot in common. But as their friendship grew and evolved to a place where I wasn't needed anymore as a connecting point between them, I felt a bit left behind. This was the moment for me to discern whether my friendliness and relatability were truly altruistic, or whether they had hidden strings attached.

I have equal capacity to be the centerpiece of things in a freeing way or in a controlling way. And I have chosen both paths over my lifetime. At times, I have been happy to be a glue player on the team that quietly does my part to keep the family together; but at other times, I have needed everyone to recognize and show gratitude for my work in curating community.

Are you the centerpiece of your communities in ways that are freeing, or in ways that are controlling? You might try a graphic way of visualizing this for yourself. Draw a circle for each community that you are a part of and identify where you fit in each community—are you at the center or at an edge?—and then identify how much room you take up in each circle. How much room is there for other people to occupy?

OVERCOMING FEAR

THE MOST CONSISTENT MESSAGE throughout the Hebrew Bible and New Testament is "do not fear." If the counters are to be believed, the encouragement to "fear not" is mentioned 365 times in the Bible. The compilers of Scripture must have known that we were going to be afraid.

Free-floating fear seems to be everywhere. As humans, we cohere around fear. As I write, I am hunkered down in my Nashville home under a stay-at-home order from my governor as we collectively do what we can to slow the spread of COVID-19. Along with the rest of the world, I'm swimming in fears of sickness, isolation, and economic uncertainty. At the same time that we as a community are focused on the coronavirus pandemic, I am adjusting to being diagnosed with multiple sclerosis in a time when I'm having to talk to my doctors by telephone or video about my diagnosis, prognosis, and treatment. I am unsettled, to say the least.

In Enneagram wisdom, Sixes are traditionally described as the "fear" number since their passion is fear. According to the Enneagram, Sixes are haunted by a wounding message that tells them that the world is full of hidden dangers and that they shouldn't trust themselves to navigate the dangers safely on their own. But there are also several other numbers beyond Sixes that deal with anxiety that is consistently present under the surface of personality.

Even though Twos wrestle with the passion of pride rather than fear, my experience of being a Two is that we experience a lot of anxiety derived from the personality that our Enneagram number describes. The difference between the anxiety that Sixes experience and the anxiety that Twos experience is in the focus of the anxiety. Sixes are anxious about car wrecks, tornadoes, snakes, and school shooters. The anxiety that Sixes experience is mostly centered around external dangers that might invade and disrupt their world. The anxiety that Twos experience is mostly centered around relationships.

I have a lot of fear around relationships. I am afraid that people are mad at me. I am afraid that I will do something or fail to do something that will cause a friendship to rupture. I'm anxious about being alone. I'm anxious when someone has a need that I can't meet. My stomach drops every time someone asks me to do something that I don't want to do, and I am invited to say the scariest two-letter word in the human language: no.

I need the Bible's encouragement about fear and anxiety. Just because I am not worried about external events like hurricanes and burglars doesn't mean that I don't have a lot of anxiety bubbling beneath the surface of my go-getter, optimistic personality.

As Twos, we are invited to name the source of our anxiety —a source which is typically relationship-focused. In naming the source, we can open our hands to the Prince of Peace, asking God to help us experience the calming confidence that only a spiritual journey can bring. Be not afraid.

"In this world you will have trouble. But take heart! I have overcome the world" (Jesus in John 16:33).

> *God, into my anxiety, come. Help me to embrace faith in you, faith in myself, and faith in the long-term stickiness of my relationships. Amen.*

MISTER ROGERS' NEIGHBORHOOD

I LOVE MR. ROGERS. When the documentary *Won't You Be My Neighbor* was released in 2018, I took my entire church staff to the theater to watch it. In 2019, I returned to the theater to watch Tom Hanks play Mr. Rogers in *A Beautiful Day in the Neighborhood*.

Toward the end of the movie, Rogers is at the bedside of a man who is dying. The man is in his last days of life, but the family gathered around his bedside isn't ready to admit that death is close. Rogers, realizing that the family wasn't prepared to name the inevitable, shared this wisdom: "What can be mentioned can be managed." He encouraged the family to embrace talking about their father's impending death, helping them to see that once it can be mentioned, the complicated emotions around death that they were all experiencing would be much easier to manage.

What can be mentioned can be managed.

This is good wisdom for all of us! As Enneagram Twos, we have spent our lifetimes undermentioning our feelings and needs. And this has made it hard for us to manage them. When people ask us what we are feeling or what we need, we shift attention away from ourselves and fail to truly divulge, to ourselves and to others, our deepest feelings and our deepest needs.

Our feelings and needs are unmentioned, which means they are unmanaged and unresolved. And unresolved feelings and needs come out sideways. They sneak up on us and take us by surprise, or they get retranslated into frustrations and resentments. Is it possible that if we let more of our feelings and needs be mentioned that we would be better able to manage them in healthy, productive ways?

What are your feelings and needs that can't be mentioned?

HUMILITY

I RECENTLY TRAVELED to Kalamazoo, Michigan, with my friend Suzanne Stabile for an Enneagram event that she was hosting at The Fetzer Institute. While Suzanne and I were in Kalamazoo, we met Sister Betsy, a nun from the Congregation of St. Joseph. Sister Betsy is one of the most winsome, delightful people I have ever met. Suzanne and I were instantly drawn to her engaging smile, her earthy humor, and her tender heart.

On our last day in Kalamazoo, Suzanne and I wanted to spend time with Sister Betsy. We asked for a tour of her convent, Nazareth House, a beautiful, sprawling structure that was slated for demolition a few months later. The order of nuns at St. Joseph had so diminished that there were no resources to keep up the grand center built for a bygone era.

Toward the end of our tour, Sister Betsy took Suzanne and me into the chapel of Nazareth House. The chapel was breathtaking in its beauty, order, and sense of transcendent presence. It was a clear testimony of years of faithful nuns and priests gathering for liturgies of prayer. As I took in the sights of the room, I noticed a recurring theme. The chapel had the image of a peacock with its feathers down as a focal depiction in its art, candle holders, and architectural elements. I almost didn't recognize the bird as a peacock because I am so used to seeing peacocks depicted with their feathers puffed up and out. I asked Sister Betsy about the meaning of a peacock with its feathers down. She told me that, in spiritual representations, the peacock with its feathers out represents pride, and the peacock with its feathers down represents humility. The imagery instantly made sense as I saw how a lifetime of formation in this chapel had transformed Sister Betsy and the other nuns into saints who practiced humility. Nuns who told us that they didn't resent the upcoming demolition of their home and way of life, but instead were looking forward to taking up a smaller carbon footprint.

As Enneagram Twos, our core passion is pride, but our corresponding invitational virtue is humility, which is the antidote to pride. Humility for Twos looks like admitting that we have needs just like everyone else. It involves taking ourselves down from the pedestal of the helper, savior, and fixer, and joining the human race of souls who are all grappling with needing to be helped, saved, and fixed.

I have a bronze figure of a peacock with its feathers down in the entry hall of my home to remind me that I become my most beautiful when I let my feathers fall down and I stop trying to convince the world that I am grand and strong. I want to be more like Sister Betsy. When a peacock has its feathers down, you don't always notice the beautiful plumes from far away, but when you get up close, you can't help but see the vibrant feathers that brush the ground.

First Peter 5:5 says, "Clothe yourselves with humility." What a great verse for us Twos to cling to in opposition to our pride!

> *God, help me to follow the example of Christ, who always chose the path of humility over pride. Forgive the ways that I puff myself up and help me to embrace the parts of me that I keep hidden away from the world. Amen.*

MARTHA IN THE KITCHEN

WHEN THE ENNEAGRAM IS APPLIED to biblical characters, Martha, the sister of Mary and Lazarus, is described as possibly being an Enneagram Two. You remember Martha, right? She's the one clanging dishes in the kitchen, hoping that Jesus and her sister, Mary, might hear her from the living room and come help. Martha took care of everybody by attending to the practical, earthy needs of the day, but like so many of us Twos, she became resentful once she realized what her overserving was costing her.

In his Gospel, Luke wrote, "Martha was distracted by her many tasks" (Luke 10:40 NRSV). Her preparations made her miss some really great moments in the living room where Jesus was teaching Mary and the others who were gathered. It all came to a boiling point when Martha finally expressed her frustration to Jesus at being left alone while everyone else was having a grand time. Unfortunately for Martha (and for all of us who resonate with her story!), Jesus wasn't buying her martyring frustration.

I feel deeply exposed by this story. So much of my life is filled with times where I am alone in kitchens of my own making while it feels like the rest of the world is savoring the joy of the moment. The parade passes by while I am meeting somebody else's needs and ignoring my own. And the whole thing gets even worse when, like Martha, I start to feel sorry for myself and finally boil over with frustration, making myself a victim of everyone else's needs that they never even asked me to meet!

What is your overserving costing you?

Who around you is taking the brunt of your resentment?

Like Martha, where have you missed the greater thing by distracting yourself with a lesser thing?

CODEPENDENCY

I DON'T WANT to just be your friend. I want to be the person about whom you might say, "I have all of these friends, but then there's *Hunter*!" Then I want you to begin describing the ways in which our friendship surpasses all of the others that you have had in your life, recounting specific times that I have surprised you by anticipating and meeting your needs before you even knew that you had them.

Are you exhausted by reading this yet? *Chad was*. In college, I learned the hard way how overbearing I can be in relationships. Relationships are everything to me, and my early life was spent curating deep and personal friendships, usually with someone who for a season would have been described as my best friend. I began to notice that after a period of time—maybe a year or two—our friendship would wane. With the benefit of hindsight and therapy, I discovered that I can be a lot for people. I want to be so close, so quickly, that I tend to dive into the deep end of friendship before the other person agrees to give me this place in their life.

One night in college, my best friend, Chad, and I were having a conflict over a trip to the beach that he was taking without me. He became exasperated and told me that my overbearingness was choking him. I was ashamed and hurt—but that night opened fertile ground for deeper awareness. I began to recognize the ways in which my desire for close friendship led to unhealthy behaviors.

Suzanne Stabile, a fellow pilgrim Two, often says in her "Know Your Number" workshops, "If God didn't mean for me to create codependent, enmeshed relationships, then why did God give me all of the tools that are necessary to do so?" To which I shout, *Yes and amen!*

As Twos, we have tendencies toward codependency, especially in close relationships. My best friends were everything to me. And I wanted to be everything to them—except that wasn't healthy for any of us. My neediness and overbearingness sabotaged several good friendships.

I am learning to recognize my orientation to pursue relationships that have markers of codependency. I am learning, slowly, to make sure that my relationships are mutual in every way, not supported by my own neediness or overpursuing. I am learning to be content as someone's friend—even someone's good friend—without needing them to let me occupy a place in their lives that is higher than all the rest of the people they love.

Take a few minutes today to meditate on relationships in your life that have ended poorly. Can you recognize in any of them times when you demanded or expected too much?

What has been your track record for being a good respecter of boundaries—your own and the boundaries of others?

INCARNATION

I'VE BEEN HELPED over the past ten years by three therapists who walked with me through important, liminal seasons of life. My belief is that all of us could benefit from the helpful companionship of mental health professionals, spiritual directors, and other guides as we navigate what it means to be human.

One of the beautifully frustrating things about my three experiences with three different counselors is that they were not content with my responses to their questions about what I was feeling at any given time. They each had a follow-up question to my "I'm feeling sad today" or "I'm feeling frustrated today." And the question was always the same . . . "Where are you feeling this in your body?"

Where am I feeling this in my body? I have no idea! It was a struggle for me to connect with my body in a deep enough way to answer this question. One time, in frustration at my own lack of self-knowledge and my therapist's persistence in asking the question, I shouted, "my elbow!" in hopes that my therapist would move on.

As a Two, I often under-recognize and under-prioritize the needs of my body. I think there are three primary culprits for this malaise: (1) my core emotion of shame, (2) my underidentification of my own needs, and (3) my over-identification with matters of the heart. All of this means that I miss body cues. I sometimes miss being hungry, and I sometimes miss being full. I sometimes miss the mounting stress accumulating in my upper shoulders until the headache sets in. Many times, I push down the anxiety that later shows up in the pit of my gut.

One of our invitations as Twos is to discover what it means to inhabit a body that has more than just a heart but that also has a mind, a gut, a back, and legs. I still struggle to answer the question of where emotions are showing up in my body, but I'm learning to trust my body more and more. I'm learning to listen to its cues and signals.

What are you feeling right now?

Where is it showing up in your body?

Take a few minutes today to practice a body scan. Find a comfortable chair to sit in and place both your feet on the floor, with legs, arms, and hands uncrossed. Close your eyes and take several deep breaths. With your eyes still closed, bring your attention to the top of your head and feel the sensation of your scalp. After several seconds, begin to move down your body, with stops at the face, the jaw, the shoulders, the arms, the chest, the stomach, the hands, the thighs, the legs, and the feet. Take five seconds at each stop to recognize different things about each particular part of your body—are you stiff, tense, tingly, or relaxed? Once you reach your feet, relax everything, take several deeper breaths, and open your eyes. What did you learn about your body?

WHAT DO WE DO
WITH OUR ANGER?

I HAVE LOTS OF SHOWER FIGHTS. Not actual fights with other human beings, but imaginary fights that occur in frantic dialogue in my mind while I shower. I often hear from other Twos that they also have shower fights, or fights in their minds when their heads hit the pillow at night, or fights in their minds as they drive to work.

When I am alone in a quiet space, like the shower, bed, or car, my mind begins racing with recollections of hurts from the day and things that I wish I had been able to say to people but never said. I give some great speeches in the shower and tell people off with the pithiest acerbic wit. *I wish you could hear me!*

In these moments, I finally notice my anger. Typically, if you ask me whether I get angry, I might say that I never feel angry. I bury my anger underneath shame and sadness. It is rare for me to experience anger in real time. Anger comes later—after the shame and sadness have settled in. Anger comes in the quiet moments, when my defenses are down and I am alone with my own scattered thoughts. But because I don't experience anger in real time, I don't process it in real time, and so it stays mostly unresolved.

Twos are often disconnected from anger, which lives behind our shame, anxiety, loneliness, and sadness. Much of our emotional experience as Twos involves misplaced anger. What if we began to ask ourselves what anger is living behind our other emotions?

If we learn to befriend our anger, we can discover what it has to teach us. Maybe our anger is trying to teach us to say no when we really don't have anything left to give. Maybe it's trying to teach us to stick up for our own needs, or maybe it's trying to teach us to be honest about our true feelings in the moment no matter the relational cost.

Our best tour guide for how to effectively process anger is our trusty friend the Enneagram Eight. Twos and Eights have a special relationship, evidenced by the line that runs between them on the Enneagram figure. The line connecting the two numbers suggests that Eights move toward Two tendencies in times of integration or security, and that Twos move toward Eight tendencies in times of disintegration or stress. The important thing for Twos to explore about this journey is to learn how we can access, in times of stress, the most helpful characteristics of an Enneagram Eight. People commonly misunderstand the Enneagram by believing that you can only access unhealthy behaviors from the number that you move toward in stress. By learning from Eights, I have discovered what it looks like for them to express anger in healthy ways. As a Two, I can choose to pick up healthy tools from Eights to take care of myself.

Over the course of the past six months, I moved, renovated my new home, left a job, experienced family stress, fractured my ankle, and was diagnosed with multiple sclerosis, a chronic disease. And did I mention that this all happened during the Thanksgiving and Christmas holidays? Over this stressful season, I saw myself fall to the bottom of Two space in unhealthy, excess behavior. For me, the bottom of my Two-ness involves such charming behaviors like feeling sorry for myself, jumping into people's lives in unhelpful ways as I try to make myself needed and necessary, and burdening loved ones with lots of chatter about how much I have given and how little I have been appreciated. When I stay at the bottom of Two long enough, I intuitively move toward Eight, my stress number.

When I make the move toward Eight subconsciously, without any intentionality, I pick up uncontrolled and free-floating anger, bitter frustration, and in rare moments, misplaced rage. If, on the other hand, I recognize the season of stress and use some of the healthier behaviors from Eight to take care of myself, I can find resilience, boundaries, and internal strength. As a Two, I am inexperienced in processing and expressing my anger, so I am learning what to do from my friends who are Eights.

If we as Enneagram Twos are going to follow James's advice to be slow to express our anger, we will need the high side of Eight to help us.

Can you recognize what Eight behaviors might be helpful for you to pick up as a Two in times of stress?

Is your anger bubbling up in circumstances that surprise you?

What might it look like for you to admit and allow your anger?

FIRST RESPONDERS

IN MID-2019, I began planning for how I might dedicate some weeks at the end of the year to a writing project. I was eager to have open space in my calendar to devote exclusively to it, free from the usual office and meeting schedules that fill my days. As the weeks for my office hiatus came closer, I became more and more excited as I anticipated the long, uninterrupted opportunity to create.

The first couple of days came and went much as I had planned. I woke early, took a morning walk, made coffee, sat at my new desk—bought especially for this endeavor—and wrote. A few days later, however, trouble came. And trouble came for me, as it always does, under the disguise of social connection.

A beloved congregant from the church that I formerly pastored died, and his wife called to ask if I would help with his funeral. Next, one of my favorite friends, who lives out of town, visited Nashville and we had lunch together. And did I mention that I was missing some of my office colleagues, so I went for coffee with one of them?

In Enneagram wisdom, Kathleen Hurley and Theodore Dobson helped us discover that Twos have a *present* orientation to time. When I first heard this, it mystified me because I don't often feel like I am tapped into any Zen present-in-the-moment bliss. As my Enneagram studies grew deeper, however, I began to understand that a present orientation to time—which is shared by all Ones, Twos, and Sixes—is more about responding to stimuli in the present than connecting to the spiritual presence of the now.

Having a present orientation to time for me means that all my plans are written in pencil, ready to be edited or erased if someone needs something from me (or appears to need something from me). I am a responder. I react to people, to feelings, to moments, to needs. And all my responding and reacting gets me off course from my goals.

So much of Enneagram wisdom reveals the mystery that the worst part of us is the best part of us, and the best part of us is the worst part. As a Two, my present orientation to time is part of what makes me emotionally intelligent, responsive in the moment, and a helpful, attentive friend. But it is also what makes me frustrated at my lack of willpower, angry at my self-sabotaging of plans and goals, and exhausted from doing so many things that weren't really the right things for me to do.

As a Two, I will always be oriented to the present—it's the best and worst of me. But, I am learning to pay attention to the past and the future. I am learning to build some accountability and boundaries in my life to keep me headed toward my goals, and I am learning to make space to integrate the past into my story as well. I am also learning to be careful to not give a yes as quickly as I once did, now that I realize that every yes has an accompanying no.

How has being present-oriented helped you, and how has it hurt you?

What might you do to bring more attention to the integration of your past and the pursuit of your goals?

God of past, present, and future, help me to pay attention to the things that are right for me today. Amen.

HOW DO WE KNOW IF
WE ARE HEALTHY?

I BELIEVE THAT ROMANS 11:29 is one of the scariest verses in the Bible. It says that God's gifts and call are "irrevocable." I understand this to mean that God gives us gifts and doesn't take them back. Our gifts are not connected to our faithfulness; they are connected to God's faithfulness. Our gifts will work even when we don't.

I love giving gifts to my five-year-old niece. I give them to her because I love her, not because she's earned them. It doesn't even cross my mind when I'm buying her Christmas gifts to wonder whether she's been good or deserving. I give her gifts because she brings me so much joy simply by existing on the planet.

God gives each of us unique gifts, but God also gives some common gifts to us as Enneagram Twos—principally gifts related to compassion, empathy, emotional intelligence, love, and kindheartedness. We use these gifts every day to help people and the communities that we belong to. And

God doesn't take these gifts away. God gives us gifts because God is faithful, not because we are faithful.

Of course, I'm exaggerating by calling Romans 11:29 scary, but I do believe that it cautions us to remember that the true test of our health and faithfulness is not whether or not the gifts inside of us work, but rather if we are representing the fruit of the Holy Spirit in everything that we do: love, joy, peace, patience, kindness, goodness, faithfulness, gentleness, and self-control (Galatians 5:22-23).

I honestly believe that God has given me a gift to teach. But Romans 11:29 tells me that I should not mistakenly believe that my motivations are healthy when I get up on a stage and successfully teach others. The true test of my spiritual health is based on how well my life is manifesting the fruit of the Holy Spirit, not how well my life is manifesting the gifts that God has given me.

As Twos, we are invited to remember that just because our gifts of serving are making a difference in the lives of people does not mean that we are healthy. We'll need to evaluate our spiritual health in other ways.

What gifts has God uniquely placed inside of you?

Can you recognize times when the gifts worked even when you were worn out or unhealthy?

What are more reliable ways for you to evaluate your emotional, physical, and spiritual health?

EXTRA! EXTRA! READ ALL ABOUT IT!

EXCESS IN MY TWO-NESS most often comes when I say yes to something when I really wanted to say no.

As I'm writing this entry, there is a conversation that I am putting off having about resigning from a committee that I have wanted to resign from for two years. When I was asked to serve on the committee five years ago, I really didn't have the time or heart for it, but because of relational connection with the person who asked me to serve, I said yes. Almost immediately, I regretted saying yes. I became angry with myself for getting into so many things that I really don't want to do just because saying no feels like it has the potential for social disconnection.

For me, excess looks like frustration, misplaced resentment, and, if I'm really having an "extra" kind of day, martyring. Martyring always represents excess for Twos; it's the bottom of the barrel. It's never pretty and it's never helpful. And martyring—which is finding connection with someone by telling them how hard I have worked or how much I have given—almost always comes when I said yes to something when I really wish I had said no.

Fortunately, excess has an antidote, and it's only a two-letter word: no. I am learning to say no in kind and honest ways so that I can protect myself and those I love from reaching the bottom of my Two-ness in resentful martyring.

"All you need to say is simply 'Yes' or 'No.'" (Matthew 5:37 NIRV).

When have you said yes when you really meant to say no?

What are your yes answers costing you?

THE BEST PART OF ME

THE AFTER-THE-PARADE BLUES. It is something that hits many of us after a day of pouring our best energy into our work, our event, or our community volunteering. For me, I call it "the Sunday blues" because it hits me most Sunday afternoons after a morning of teaching Sunday school, preaching a sermon, and connecting with church members after the service. I get into the car and the blues begins to settle in as I drive from the church parking lot. Whatever our work—whether it's something we get paid to do or something we simply choose to give—there is a moment when the parade is over, the balloons have deflated, and the confetti is on the ground . . . that is when the blues can take over.

For me, the Sunday blues is a tired melancholy that makes me extra sensitive and emotionally needy. Doesn't that sound fun to be around?! The source of the blues is plain and simple exhaustion. All the connecting that my work requires takes a toll on me physically, mentally, and emotionally.

Many people who aren't Twos mistakenly believe that Twos are all extroverts, that Twos have an endless supply of energy for connecting, and that Twos love to be with people all the time. None of this is true, however—especially for me as a Two that trends more introverted than extroverted.

The problem with my Sunday blues is that the people I love the most get the worst version of me. The people to whom I want to give my best get the *tired me*. Too often, I give my best to the crowd and then am left with my extra-sensitive, needy, and melancholy self by the time I get to the ones that I long to connect with the most.

There are two questions that I am learning to ask myself about the Sunday blues—which, of course, can come for me on Mondays, Tuesdays, Wednesdays, Thursdays, Fridays, and Saturdays. First: How can I take the time to re-center myself so that when I engage with my loved ones, I have a healthy, refreshed self to give them rather than a worn-out, burned-out self? And second: How can I manage what I give emotionally and physically so that I don't give everything to the crowd, but instead leave some good stuff for the people at home who deserve my intention and attention?

Too often for Twos, our loved ones get the worst versions of us. We're out chasing connections, winning the crowd over, and "saving" everyone's days, while the people we love the most are waiting to see if we have saved some of our connecting energy for them. Our invitation is to make sure that we spend our energy in the right places by giving the people we love the most *our best*.

Are your family members and closest friends continually getting the exhausted version of you?

Consider this guided meditation practice for the next time you sense the blues settling in: Close your eyes for five to ten minutes and visualize yourself hiking your favorite trail. Imagine that toward the end of the trail, there is a new split-off toward a path that you have never walked before. Imagine yourself choosing the new path. Follow its steep, winding ascent through new terrain and landscape that you haven't seen before. Finally, the path reaches a summit and at the top, imagine that Jesus is waiting for you. Visualize him, smell him, see him, touch him, and hear him ask you: "What can I do for you?" What is your answer?

LOVE, HENRI

HENRI NOUWEN WAS a Catholic priest and prolific author who spent the last years of his life living as a spiritual director in a residential living facility for adults with intellectual disabilities. As a self-identified Two, he is a patron saint for many of us.

I have read a lot of Nouwen's books and shared my love for him with my friend Darin, also an Enneagram Two. Recently, Nouwen's estate released a final work, his collected letters, titled *Love, Henri*. I knew that this book was preparing for publication and Darin and I talked about it on a trip that we took to Chattanooga the fall before its release. The day that *Love, Henri* was released, Darin bought us both copies and put mine in the mail to Nashville. I opened it immediately and began to read. A third of the way through *Love, Henri*, I put it down and haven't picked it up again.

Reading someone's personal letters is very different than reading someone's edited manuscripts. *Love, Henri* is a wonderful collection that reveals much of Nouwen's thoughts, feelings, and motivations, but it hit too close to home for me.

What I discovered was that Nouwen had an arc to many of his letters that included three parts: a gushy beginning, the contents of what he needed to share, and a gushy ending.

Nouwen's letters reveal a person who spent his life longing for deep connection in a religious system that didn't allow him to experience connection in all of the ways that he longed for. Many of his letters focus mainly on affirmations of connection and requests for future connection, leaving little room for much more.

I felt exposed by *Love, Henri* because so much of my life is spent looking for connection, soliciting connection, and inviting others to affirm the eternal bonds of our connections. I suspect that Nouwen, like me, struggled to find contentment and permanency in his connections. I suspect that Nouwen, like me, overconnected with the people that he loved—especially through his affectionate letters—because he wondered at the end of the day if there was truly anyone to whom he belonged.

As Twos, we are often visited by the existential questions of belonging and connection. And even though we connect easily with people, many of us struggle with loneliness and questions of whether the other person feels as strongly about us as we feel about them.

Because our gift as Twos is social connection, many of our problems come from our social connections. Both-and. Shadow and light. Nouwen was beloved by the world but was still haunted in the dark night of his soul with questions of love and belonging. In his book *In the Name of Jesus,*

Nouwen wrote: "I began to ask myself whether my lack of contemplative prayer, my loneliness, and my constantly changing involvement in what seemed most urgent were signs that the Spirit was gradually being suppressed."

The features of our personalities that represent our best lights are also the features that create trouble for us. We are invited to embrace the mystery of this paradox.

Give yourself an extra dose of compassion today knowing that you're in good company. We all live in the mystery of the both-and.

As we continue to build new spiritual practices into our lives, consider this method of incorporating a daily examen at the end of your day. Every evening (when I take the time and remember), I write one sentence based on the prompt, "From this day, I remember . . ." Daily journaling is too much for me to realistically commit to long-term, so I started keeping a journal entry on my phone with the "From this day, I remember" prompt. Some days I skip it; some days I write one word; and some days I write several sentences. The idea is to begin taking inventory of what dominated my thoughts and memories from the day. Every few months, I scan the entries from the past season to recognize core emotions and important stories, and to notice what is looming large in my life. For me, the "From this day, I remember" method of a daily review is simple, quick, and helpful in naming my feelings, needs, hopes, and fears.

THINK!

A COUPLE OF YEARS AGO on a trip to Texas, my friend Dave Larlee, pastor of All Saints Church in Dallas—and most importantly, a fellow Enneagram Two—shared with me his latest mantra: "Facts are my friends."

Twos make decisions from the heart and over-rely on feelings to determine what we think. If I'm honest with myself, many of the ways that I decide how I should spend my days, what I should buy, and what I should eat are based on feelings—my own and the feelings of other people.

Dave's mantra is such a good one for me as a Two who over-relies on feelings and under-relies on facts. Enneagram wisdom, based on the teaching of Kathleen Hurley and Theodore Dobson, says that Twos are thinking-repressed. When I first heard this idea, it didn't resonate with me because, like all of us, I spend my days thinking. The problem is that most of my thinking is about feelings and relationships. And my thoughts about feelings and relationships are not always productive or true.

Recently, I exchanged a series of text messages with someone I have been friends with for years. This friend and

I have shared trips together, meals together, and so much of the good and bad of life together. And yet, over the span of fifty words, I decided that this friend was upset with me—even though he said that he wasn't! And because I decided that he was upset with me, I also decided that we probably wouldn't be close any longer. For two days, I quietly spiraled over the grieving realization that I had lost a friend because we exchanged two terse text messages in a space where both of us were exhausted and overspent. A week later, my friend reached out to me and we picked up the friendship right where we had left off. There was no damage and no breaking. All of the problems had been in my mind.

If I had taken a moment to move from my unproductive thinking, which was really just made up of feelings, to look at the facts, I could have seen that this person is a steady, longtime friend; that this person explicitly told me that he was not upset with me; and that we were speaking over text messages, which notoriously sound snappier than they are intended to sound.

Facts are our friends!

> As you move through days filled with feelings and relationships, and thoughts about feelings and relationships, include facts by asking yourself: "Is what I am feeling true and supported by the facts?"

WHAT DO WE DO WITH OUR SUFFERING?

RECENTLY, AS I WAS PREPARING to preach, I came to a familiar passage in Romans 5 in which Paul writes: "We also boast in our sufferings, knowing that suffering produces endurance, and endurance produces character, and character produces hope, and hope does not disappoint us, because God's love has been poured into our hearts through the Holy Spirit that has been given to us" (Romans 5:3-5 NRSV). I began to order a sermon around the roadmap from suffering to hope, with stops of endurance and character along the way.

My initial thoughts and preparations were all around discovering the formula for moving from suffering to endurance, and the pattern for getting from endurance to character, and the steps to take us from character to hope. I was stumped, however, by the passive language of "produces," which implies that suffering naturally produces endurance, and endurance naturally produces character, and character naturally produces hope. As I progressed in putting the sermon together, I began to sense that this was a journey that the Spirit did in us—producing endurance, character, and hope. It didn't sound like we had much to do at all with the process.

Except for one thing: *don't avoid the suffering!* I discovered through my study of Romans 5 that the only formula, pattern, or step for us to take in the journey from suffering to hope is to not avoid the suffering.

I have so many tricks for avoiding suffering, and I bet that you do too. I can eat something, buy something, watch something, or—the favorite trick of all for Twos—find someone to help. As Twos, we avoid our own suffering by identifying with the suffering of other people. We minimize our own suffering by attending to the suffering of people we love. The problem is that, when it comes to our own lives, we don't have as much endurance, character, or hope as we would like to have.

The only way that we will make it safely down the road from suffering to hope is to pay attention to our own suffering. As Twos, we need to learn to stop minimizing our own needs, our own longings, our own losses, and our own disappointments. If we can begin to allow our own suffering to get the attention that we have given to the suffering of everyone else, we will see the Spirit build endurance, character, and hope in us. And hope does not disappoint.

What are the numbing strategies that you regularly turn to in order to avoid or alleviate suffering?

God of hope, help us to acknowledge and offer up our suffering so that your Spirit can build endurance, character, and hope in us. Amen.

THE 80/20 RULE

I WENT TO A LEADERSHIP conference in 2014 where a facilitator said something that has affected the way that I think about leadership ever since: "If someone can do something 80 percent as well as you can, bless them to do it." The facilitator was referring to ways that we avoid delegating and releasing things that really should be delegated and released because we tell ourselves that no one can do *the thing* as well as we can.

This is not only great wisdom for leaders, it's also great wisdom for Enneagram Twos. We respond quickly to needs around us. But for every yes there is an accompanying no, and every time that we swoop in to help, there is someone else who wasn't able to help. We take up a lot of the helper spaces in life. And not only do we keep other people from helping, but also, we keep people from helping themselves.

My pride makes me want to become indispensable to people, which means that it is hard for me to free up a space for someone else to fill. One of the challenges of pastoring was creating a preaching calendar that included people other than myself. I knew that it was good for the congregation to hear other voices, and that it was good for other voices to have opportunities to share their obvious giftings, but I had to overcome my desire to fill every gap and plug every hole.

When we don't make room for other people to jump in, two negative things occur: we keep other people from their gifts, and we keep ourselves from the work that is truly ours.

I'm learning to ask myself, "Is this something that only I can or *will* do?" And if the answer is an honest "no," I'm slowly learning to bless someone else to do it while also blessing myself *not* to do it!

How have your helping actions created obstacles for other people to bring their gifts to the table?

How have your rescue efforts kept other people dependent on you?

What have you left undone while you were busy doing things that weren't yours to do?

GO, GO, GO JOSEPH!

JOSEPH IS ONE of the most dynamic characters in the Bible. At the beginning of Joseph's story, we meet him as the misunderstood romantic in his family. He was his father's favorite son, and his mother was his father's favorite wife. His dad, Jacob, wanted everyone to know just how unique and special Joseph was by giving him a multicolored, show-stopping coat. This special attention didn't earn Joseph any admiration from his brothers, who surely felt overlooked in the company of Jacob's special son. To make matters worse for himself, Joseph had a gift: he saw things in dreams and visions that other people didn't see.

I know that you're not supposed to type people with Enneagram numbers, but let's look at Joseph's story and see if we can discover the ways in which he follows some of the personality patterns of an Enneagram Four. Like all Enneagram Fours, Joseph saw color where the rest of the world saw black and white. And because Joseph was young and his gifts were not tempered by age or wisdom, he shared his dreams and visions with his brothers, even when the visions were of his brothers' crops bowing down and worshiping his own. Finally, Joseph's brothers had had enough, and they tried to kill him.

As the story progressed, Joseph attended the school of hard knocks. His brothers tried to kill him. He was sold into slavery. He was seduced and lied about by a powerful woman. He was thrown into jail. The future looked bleak for Joseph in every way. But, Joseph got a break because of his gift for dream interpretation. He was able to interpret one of Pharaoh's dreams, which saved Egypt from years of famine, and he was chosen to become Pharaoh's right-hand man.

Toward the end of Joseph's story, his brothers came groveling for food to Pharaoh's assistant, but they didn't recognize the assistant as their long-lost brother—and finally the moment for Joseph's revenge was nigh! Joseph could have taken the revenge he was owed, but, tempered by age and wisdom, he instead showed mercy to his brothers and ended up saving the entire lineage of Israel from dying by famine.

The beautiful evolution depicted by Joseph's story is one of a person who early in life was preoccupied with his own special story, but later in life found his place in the story of his family—not as the special son, but as an important part of the group. One of the invitations for Enneagram Fours is to find their place in a story that is bigger than their own story. Joseph points the way to this path of transformation.

If you are familiar with the Enneagram figure, you may have noticed that there is a line connecting Twos with Fours. The school of the Enneagram that I principally learn and teach from, embodied by my mentor Suzanne Stabile and standing in the tradition of much of the Jesuit teaching of the Enneagram, believes that this line represents a move that Twos make toward Four behavior in secure and integrated moments. When Twos are in the ruts of life—or in the groove, as I like to say—we migrate toward Four behavior to get some extra characteristics and actions.

The problem is that we can go get behaviors from Four that are helpful to our pursuit of meaning, belonging, and vocation in times of integration and security or we can pick up things from Four that hurt us more than help us. When I as a Two pick up unhelpful Four behaviors, I become preoccupied with my own story. In these moments, I feel like I am the victim of circumstance, just like young Joseph. I may feel like nobody sees me for who I truly am and that no one appreciates my unique, special gifts.

But we can choose a higher path. We can move toward Four and find our place in a story that is bigger than our own story—a larger human story that includes our stories as well as the stories of others.

Can you see how both helpful and unhelpful Four behaviors show up in your life when you move toward Four behaviors in security?

Are you preoccupied with your own story? When is it hard for you to detach from your own perspective long enough to truly empathize with others around you?

What can you learn from observing your friends and loved ones who are Fours about how to move toward Four in helpful, not harmful, ways?

FINDING HOPE

ON THE FIRST SUNDAY OF ADVENT in churches that observe liturgical practices, it's traditional to light a candle to represent hope. This year, as I sat through the service dedicated to celebrating the hope that Advent brings, I found it hard to hope. I was sitting in the middle of grief, the uncertainty of being between jobs, and the fear that some of the demons of anxiety and depression that have accompanied me through life may have been emerging from dormancy.

"Hope deferred makes the heart sick," the Bible says in Proverbs 13:12. For me, when hope is deferred, then anger, bitterness, and cynicism fill its place. As Twos, the wounding message we have experienced teaches us to be helpful, cheerful, and hopeful. We don't want attention to be focused on our needs—especially our hopelessness. I find it hard to be honest with people when I feel hopeless. Typically, I end every negative thing that I say with something like, "but it's all okay" or "I'll be better tomorrow."

The problem is that when I lose touch with my negative emotions, like hopelessness, I become angry, bitter, and cynical. And because I don't lead very often with negative emotions, I am not practiced with these emotions, which means that they come out sideways. Either I misdirect them toward people who don't deserve my anger, or I keep them bottled inside, creating a stew of resentment.

I am learning to recognize that when anger, bitterness, and cynicism bubble up in me, I have lost touch with hope. Instead of transferring hopelessness into anger, what if I attended to the sadness that I'm really feeling? Our loved ones would rather us be honest about the times when it is hard for us to cling to hope than for us to boil with undefined anger.

The good news about hope is that it is one of the things that remains forever, with faith and love (1 Corinthians 13). Hope doesn't run out. If you have lost it, it will come back around again. If you are finding it difficult in this season to have hope about the many things or the few things, find ways to be honest in your hopelessness so that hope deferred doesn't turn into anger, bitterness, or cynicism.

God of hope, into our darkness, come. Amen.

WINNING THEM OVER

WHEN I WAS IN FOURTH GRADE, I had one of my first experiences of being bullied. I was in the children's chorus of *The Music Man* staged by Belmont University in Nashville. I loved theater and had acted on the stage from a young age, guided by my father and grandfather, who were charismatic leading men. There were two other boys in the children's chorus, both two years older than me. I was an easy punching bag. Over the weeks of rehearsals, they made fun of me, embarrassed me in front of the other actors, and called me all the names you can imagine.

My response as an Enneagram Two? Try to win them over, of course! After several failed attempts to curtail the bullying, I started offering them the food my mom had packed for me for dinner. And then I started collecting candy bars to give to them. Finally, several Snickers bars later, I think they felt sorry enough for me because of my inability to fight back and turned their attention away from me. I spent the rest of the time in rehearsals and performances trying to earn their friendship, which was never won.

As Twos, we are people people. We have an innate desire to get other people to like us. And for the most part, people do like us. Our emotional intelligence and helpfulness attract others to us—this is part of our gift.

But there are always those people who don't like us. And I hate that! One thing that I have learned from pastoring is that every church has an antagonist. Sometimes I found that antagonist focused on me.

It is important for Twos to recognize what we do when we meet someone that we can't win over. If we can be honest with ourselves about how we respond when we encounter antagonists, we can choose healthier paths that are more honoring to ourselves.

I can recognize a pattern in my life where I dishonor myself by trying to win over my antagonists. Unfortunately, this pattern didn't stop for me in my fourth-grade theater group—it continued into my life as a pastor and beyond. I have made myself the joke before others could make it. I have gone out of my way to win over people who have shown me in a hundred ways that they are uninterested in being won over. And each time that I have gone after an antagonist, I have given something of myself up. I have diminished my own needs, my own feelings, and my own interests to try to make other people comfortable. And it has cost me a lot.

"Jesus said to them, 'A prophet is not without honor except in his own town, among his relatives and in his own home'" (Mark 6:4).

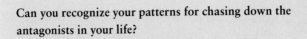

Can you recognize your patterns for chasing down the antagonists in your life?

What has it cost you?

What might it look like for you to believe that you are worthy of love and belonging even if someone else doesn't recognize your worthiness?

God, help me to love myself so that I can love you and my neighbor well. Amen.

THE FRUIT OF LOVE

IN GALATIANS 5, Paul writes that the fruit of the Holy Spirit is love, joy, peace, patience, kindness, goodness, faithfulness, gentleness, and self-control. In Matthew 7, Jesus taught how to discern between true and false prophets: "Watch out for false prophets. They come to you in sheep's clothing, but inwardly they are ferocious wolves. By their fruit you will recognize them. . . . Every good tree bears good fruit, but a bad tree bears bad fruit. . . . Thus, by their fruit you will recognize them" (Matthew 7:15-20).

The fruit of the Spirit is established through Scripture as an important test for healthy spirituality. My life, and I'm guessing yours as well, is a mixed record of good fruit and bad fruit, hopefully leaning toward the good. I carry prayer beads with me, made by my friend and fellow Enneagram Two Mike George, that include nine beads—one for each of the Galatians 5 fruits. When I pull them from my pocket to glide my hand across each of the nine beads, there are several that commonly trip me up. I believe that the beads for love, joy, and self-control offer some special invitations for me and for all Enneagram Twos, so I am devoting the next three days to these three fruits by exploring the challenges and opportunities that Two-ness presents to exhibiting love, joy, and self-control. I would invite you to meditate on the fruit of the Spirit to determine which ones cause your heart to stop and question whether the Spirit's invitation in this season is to fertilize and grow.

Love is something that Twos know a lot about. We love to love. We love to be loved. We long for relationships that move beyond casual connections and into love, intimacy, and commitment. On the surface, it seems like Enneagram Twos have the love thing figured out. We should get an A+ in the evaluation of whether the fruit of love is growing from our trees, right? *Well, not so fast!*

I have found that because I value love so highly, it is incredibly difficult for me to love people who don't love me. My faith tradition teaches me to love my enemies and to bless those who persecute and despise me, but that is a major challenge for me as a Two. Because Twos are the number that is hungriest for love, we are also the number that has a harder time than all the other numbers at loving the people who don't love us.

As Enneagram Twos, we are among the best at love, but where there is light, there is shadow. Being among the best at valuing and promoting love means that we are among the worst at clinging to love for the people who refuse to love us. When I encounter someone who simply can't or won't be won over, instead of leaning into the kingdom values of love and forgiveness, too often I quietly punish the person who refused to love me through obvious indifference, inattention, or passive aggression. This is an area of growth for me.

How can we love our neighbors as ourselves, love our enemies, pray for those who curse us, and bless those who persecute us if we don't intentionally attend to growing the fruit of love on our trees, even for those who don't love us back?

Who are the people who haven't shown you love?

If you are ready to release yourself from the prison of hate, pray for God to grow love for them on your tree. You can use the following simple prayer:
God of love, into my bitterness, resentment, hurt, and hate, come. Amen.

HAPPY DAYS ARE
HERE AGAIN

I'VE GOT THE JOY, joy, joy, joy down in my heart! *Except when I don't.*

Joy is a fruit of the Spirit that is one of the most coveted spiritual conditions. We all want joy. We recognize that happiness is fleeting and that the desire of our hearts is for the steady joy that transcends the failures and successes of life.

I have discovered, in my own journey, that joy only comes and only lasts when I am true to myself in every way—when my feelings, needs, failures, gifts, and struggles are owned by me and offered to those I love in honest and transparent ways, naked and not ashamed.

As Enneagram Twos, so much of our story is hidden from view. A mixture of pride and shame causes us to blanket our deepest truths under a cover of "I'm fine, tell me how you are doing today!" Joy is elusive, so we've settled for happiness, which requires an endless parade of connections, relationships, outings with friends, and adventures. When we are forced to be alone with our own unresolved thoughts, feelings, and needs, we will recognize the absent companion of joy.

Joy will only grow from our trees as we honor ourselves by living openly and transparently. As we make our needs known and let people into the honest truths of our complicated, mixed stories—freeing ourselves from being the hero and savior of everyone's day—we will begin to taste the beautiful gift of lasting joy.

Can you recognize ways that your Two-ness has limited the growth of joy in your life?

What is one way today that you can bear out a little bit more of your truth?

OUT OF CONTROL

SELF-CONTROL IS A FRUIT of the Spirit that is tricky for many of us Twos. Our difficulties with self-control come from misguided attempts to balance the ways in which we have denied ourselves. In public and in relationships, we practice self-denial as we prioritize other people's needs above our own, play the role of the happy helper, and extend empathetic listening to strangers and loved ones alike. But these little denials that add up throughout the day invite an opposite and equal reaction that can develop into self-indulgence.

After a day of "playing the Two," I come home exhausted and spent. I intuitively want to compensate for my exhaustion by filling myself up with something. Often this takes the form of food and I'll treat myself to something sweet to reward myself for my day. Other times my indulgence takes the form of venting, complaining, and martyring to someone who will mercifully listen to my inventory of everything that I have accomplished in the last twelve hours.

Self-control is only possible when we treat ourselves well. When self-care is abandoned, self-control fails. There is always a tendency for us to bring balance to our lives. When we overspend on behalf of others, we will overconsume, in whatever form is personal to us, on behalf of ourselves.

If the fruit of the Spirit of self-control is going to grow from our trees, we must recognize and name the ways that our overdoing is connected to our overindulging. When we are introspective and honest enough to own our lack of self-control in food, venting, sex, drinking, or spending, we can discover healthier ways to make sure that our needs are met, which usually means not denying them in the first place!

What are the symptoms of lack of self-control in your own life? Make a list and set it in front of God as a form of confession.

UNMET EXPECTATIONS

RECENTLY, I ATTENDED a meeting with a group of people that I know and love, but they were meeting five hundred miles away from my home in Nashville. I joined the meeting via a video chat service but was plagued by spotty internet connections, which meant that the video kept freezing and the audio cut out irregularly. *Not exactly the makings of a great meeting, right?* To make matters worse, I joined the meeting late, after most of the group had already met for several hours, and everyone was ready to call it a day by that time.

Things got right down to business. And because of the audio and video problems, my opportunity to hear all that was said and meaningfully engage in the conversation was limited. We moved through the agenda items quickly and wrapped up the meeting in less than an hour.

My energy went down fast during the course of the meeting and by the end, I was somber and heartsick. I got up from my desk and began asking myself why I felt so down in the dumps. I realized that I was disappointed because the meeting, full of people I love and care for as friends, was not *relational.*

The meeting, as it was intended to be, was efficient and successful in fulfilling the agenda items that needed to be accomplished. Nothing was wrong with the gathering or the participants, but lots of things were wrong with my expectations.

Expectations can get me into trouble. Anne Lamott once quipped, "Expectations are resentments under construction." I have found this to be absolutely true. I had expectations that were unrealistic and inappropriate for the session. I brought expectations of friendship and connection to a business meeting. This is one of my ongoing struggles as a Two: realizing that it is okay for some interactions, even with people I care about, to be efficient and business-like when the purpose of the meeting is not relational connection.

If I had thought before the meeting and named what I was really expecting from the participants, I could have recognized that what I was expecting was not mutually agreed on and that it was unrealistic to expect the time to evolve into a personal sharing session.

As Twos, we want things to be relational. And this is part of our beautiful gift. But when we let our relational desires come into our business interactions, we will be disappointed, and our expectations will be unmet. We are invited to name our expectations and ask ourselves: Are these expectations appropriate, and are they mutually agreed on? If the answer is no to either question, we are setting ourselves up for disappointment.

How have your expectations gone unmet recently?

Which of those expectations were perhaps inappropriate or not mutually agreed on?

SECRETS

ONE OF THE THINGS I have learned about myself in my thirty-five years of life is that I am not always the best secret keeper. This is embarrassing to admit, especially as a pastor and attorney who makes a career listening to the confidences of others. It is something that I think about daily as friends, congregants, and clients intimately confide in me.

I have come to discover that one of the primary culprits for my limited ability to keep a secret is that I am a verbal processor. And I'm guessing that if you are a Two, you're probably a verbal processor as well. I have to hear myself say something before I know if I agree with it or not! My need to verbally process is connected to the fact that Twos are thinking repressed, which is a problem for all of us who are Enneagram Ones, Twos, or Sixes.

In the times when I have betrayed someone's confidence and told their secret, it was sometimes because, like all of us, I wanted to make a connection with someone through a salacious piece of gossip. But most of the time when I have betrayed someone's confidence, it was because I needed to verbally process in order to discover how I felt about the news, what I thought about the news, and what, if anything, I was going to do based on the news.

I'm such a verbal processor that I prefer dictating to writing. On several occasions that have had to be frustrating to my long-suffering assistant, Amanda, I have asked her to read me my emails and type my dictated responses.

Sometimes my talking gets me into trouble because I say things that I don't really mean or didn't intend to share as I verbally process my way to discovering what I truly think. In being honest with myself about my processing style, I am learning to stop and think before I speak. I am also making sure to verbally process news at the right times and with the right people.

Some Twos who are dominant in the self-preserving instinctual subtype may not verbally process as much as Twos who are social dominant or sexual dominant (you can learn more about subtypes from Beatrice Chesnut's *The Complete Enneagram: 27 Paths to Greater Knowledge*). But most of us have had that experience of saying something we regret. What sorts of contexts are most likely to lead to sharing things that you later wish you hadn't shared?

One way for verbal processors to explore internal processing is through journaling. The next time that you feel the need to process your feelings and thoughts with another person, spend a few minutes journaling instead. This will help you organize what at first may seem scattered. After journaling, you may find the impulse to verbally process is lessened.

LOSING TOUCH

ONE OF MY GREAT REGRETS of life is that too often I lose touch with friends once we no longer live in the same city. When I am near someone, I'm consistently a good friend. My deepest relationships at any given moment are with people I work with, go to church with, or run into on a regular basis.

In my life so far, I have lived in North Carolina, Kentucky, New York, England, and Tennessee, and in each place, I have been blessed with robust, close relationships—friendships that at the time I could have never imagined waning. Because I live in Tennessee now, I am sad to say that many of the people I love from my seasons in North Carolina, Kentucky, New York, and England are friends that I have either lost touch with completely or only talk to once every year or two.

As Enneagram Twos, our dominant orientation to time is the present. We give our best energy to people and events that are right in front of us. This is why we are good responders. We get drawn deeply into fun events and crises of the present moment. The problem with a dominant orientation to the present is that the past and future are underrepresented in our stories.

One of the principal ways that my life has underemphasized an orientation to time of the past is that I lose too many close relationships from my past. I am so integrated into my present environment that I forget to reserve time and energy for people I love from my past. This has come at a great cost, because you can't make old friends. I am usually late to recognize these losses, again, because I am so immersed in my current circumstances.

The Enneagram helpfully points out that the pasts and futures of Twos will be naturally underrepresented in our lives unless we intentionally learn to bring more balance to past, present, and future in our orientation to time.

What old friends have you lost touch with because your attention has been so focused on your present environment?

What are some ways in which you can get out of balance in regard to your orientation to time?

ONE SIZE DOESN'T FIT ALL

IN COLLEGE, I experienced a rich season of spiritual growth. This growth was incubated by an evangelical campus ministry focused on discipleship and small-group communities that met weekly. Hundreds of miles away from my parents and the churches of my childhood, I was able to explore new spiritual questions and new spiritual practices in community with other college students who all were experimenting with forming a faith of their own.

One of the hallmarks of this campus ministry was teaching college students how to have a daily quiet time consisting of a prescribed way of studying a Scripture passage by journaling observations, interpretations, and applications. The ideal for a quiet time was to wake up early in the morning and spend time studying the Bible before classes began for the day.

I was never the best personal discipleship student. I always looked for someone to be my Bible study buddy. On days when I couldn't find anyone to journal with, I struggled to complete the quiet time on my own—not to mention that I'm not a morning person!

Before I learned the Enneagram, I didn't have any language to help me name why it was hard for me to enjoy solitary spiritual practices. Now I have language to help me understand why Ones, Twos, and Sixes—whose social style is predominantly dependent—are generally oriented to participate in spiritual practices that happen in community rather than practices that are designed to be done alone. This is why I prefer to do centering prayer in a room with other people who are also practicing centering prayer, even though it is a practice that is performed in silence.

The Enneagram illuminates the different ways that we prefer spiritual practice. Dependent numbers (Ones, Twos, and Sixes) move toward relationship and community in practicing their spirituality; withdrawing numbers (Fours, Fives, and Nines) are better able to experience robust spiritual awakening on their own, drawing from a rich interior experience; and aggressive numbers (Threes, Sevens, and Eights) are less interested in spiritual practices that involve study, thinking, and feeling, and are more interested in spiritual practices that involve productive and efficient doing— they want to experience their faith in action. In my college ministry, I'm guessing that the aggressive stance numbers were working at a soup kitchen line while the rest of us were practicing Bible study at home.

Spiritual practice is not one-size-fits-all. We need spiritual practices that are intuitive for us as well as ones that are hard for us. Since introducing Enneagram wisdom into my life, I have learned to extend more compassion to myself when spiritual practices like solitary quiet times are hard for me. I have also learned that I need spiritual practices that are hard for me because they draw me out of my traditional rhythms and invite me to discover new things about myself and God. As a pastor and spiritual teacher, I am learning to remember that we all have different entry points into the spiritual journey.

What are the easiest ways for you to practice your spirituality?

What practices are hard for you?

How have you experienced spiritual growth through practices that are both intuitive for you and ones that take more work?

GENDER AND THE ENNEAGRAM

ONE OF THE COMMON questions asked at Enneagram retreats that I lead is whether gender has anything to do in determining your Enneagram number. People are naturally interested in discovering whether certain Enneagram types are more prevalent among men or women. And, while gender does not seem to be predictive of Enneagram type, gender is an important topic in Enneagram wisdom.

American culture—and particularly the Southern American culture that I was raised in—does not always set a place at the table for every Enneagram type to manifest in maleness and femaleness. Male Twos (a club in which I'm a proud card carrier!) can have a difficult time finding cultural validation for the tenderness, sensitivity, and identification with feelings that are intuitive to our Enneagram type. Culturally, our society has not championed men who are feelers and empaths. Instead, many of us who are male Twos have sensed, from a young age, that our caregivers and friends wanted us to be a little less tender, a little more resilient, and a little tougher. For every time in my life that someone has said, "Don't take this personally," you can rest assured that I did take it personally!

Culturally, women who are Twos shoulder a different burden: one that tells them that all their helpfulness, sensitivity, and self-sacrifice are exactly how they should respond to every person and every situation. Our society often encourages female Twos to grow their personalities by over-relying on some of the unhealthiest aspects of Two-ness: namely, giving without boundaries. Women who aren't Twos also sometimes tell me that they feel like they have had to pretend to be Twos in a culture that expects women to be self-sacrificing and helpful, whether that really fit with their true personalities or not.

The beautiful gift offered by the Enneagram in this conversation about gender is the ability to name the places where culture undervalues (as is the case for male Twos) or overvalues (as is the case for female Twos) certain personality types. The Enneagram has given me confidence to embrace my Two-ness. As I have met other men who are Twos, I have become better able to embrace the gifts that come with being emotionally intelligent and naturally nurturing. The Enneagram has given me freedom to ignore the lies that I used to believe about myself: that I should be less of a feeler or I should be tougher. I've learned to stop "should-ing" on myself and to celebrate my gifts!

Whatever your gender identity, the Enneagram paves the way toward greater compassion by helping Twos realize that our personalities embody unending potential for genuine kindness, empathetic listening, and attentive helpfulness. How great would the world be if we used the wisdom of the Enneagram to set a place at the table for everybody to inhabit the personality type that is truly theirs! The Enneagram has the potential to free us from the harmful idea that there are socially acceptable and less socially acceptable Enneagram numbers for men and women. Before learning the Enneagram, I felt like I had to push down my personality—but now that I have the Enneagram, I celebrate my personality.

What messages—affirming and nonaffirming—has your community and culture communicated about your gender and your Enneagram type?

Can you recognize other gender and Enneagram pairings that don't always have a place set at the table for them? How can we go about setting places at our tables for everyone to be who they were truly made to be?

CALL ME ANYTIME

"UNDER-PROMISE AND OVER-DELIVER" is a good strategy for success in life and business, but as an Enneagram Two, I find that too often in relationships—particularly, new friendships—I have a tendency to over-promise and under-deliver. It is said that Twos are always on the make, looking to welcome new friends into their stable of connections. This has been true in my life. When I first meet someone, there is a genuine interest in sparking a new connection. Because I am good at listening and asking thoughtful questions, initial encounters with people can go very deep, very quickly. Twos invite people to close conversation earlier than most other Enneagram numbers do. To underscore this through a metaphor: we kiss on the first date!

Over time, I have become aware of how confusing this can be for people who interpret the close connection we had at an initial meeting as an invitation to a significant friendship that involves all of the expected aspects of intimacy—most especially, quality time. In connection with my pastoring, I met a fellow pastor of a church out-of-state who was burned up and worn out. The years of filling a role had left him with few places where he could share his true self. He felt truncated and alone. In our initial meeting, I was drawn to his transparency and kindness. We encouraged one another and exchanged emails. Over the course of the next couple of years, we had a few limited contacts over the phone and when he visited Nashville for conferences. What quickly became apparent was that I had not done a good job in our initial encounters of being honest about the time that I had to invest—he expected more than I had to give.

Replies like "Sure, call me anytime," "I would love to see you when you're next in town," "Of course, I would be interested in helping with that," and "Just let me know what you need" roll off my lips. And I genuinely mean these things. I wish that I had the time and energy to truly be the person who is always available to all the people I care about. But I don't. No one does. And so, I find myself in the trap where I have over-promised and under-delivered.

This is a tricky thing for us as Twos because we need to find the balance between being genuinely open and empathetic in the early moments of connection and being true to ourselves and the people who especially need our fullness. Twos need to give signals about what we honestly have to offer. Establishing right and healthy expectations for ourselves and others in relationships is a Benedictine journey of falling down and getting back up again all throughout our lives.

How do you recognize this pattern of over-promising and under-delivering in your life and relationships?

God, into our over-promising, come. Into our under-delivering, come. Help us to honor ourselves. Help us to give selflessly to the people you have called us to love. Fill us full with the gifts of the Holy Spirit of wisdom and discernment. Amen.

HEALTHY RELATIONSHIPS

EVEN TWOS GET TIRED! I've written quite a bit about how Twos love people and want to make new relationships, but if you're like me, you also have seasons of life where you want to batten down the hatches and keep everyone out. I'm fortunate to have lots of conversations with people who know their Enneagram number, and I'm discovering more and more Twos in the second half of their lives who tell me that they don't feel like Twos anymore. Some of these Twos even mistakenly tell me that they feel like they have changed their number, which isn't actually possible according to Enneagram wisdom, from being a dependent number (Ones, Twos, and Sixes, who focus on the outer world of relationships and connections) to being a withdrawing number (Fours, Fives, and Nines, who focus on the inner world of private thoughts and feelings). They feel overextended and in need of a break from their lifetimes of helping and relating.

When Twos reach these seasons of feeling exhausted and incapable of adding any more relationships, we have opportunities for reflection. This is both good news and bad news.

The good news is that we can grow by spending time alone. When we travel alone, practice spirituality alone, or simply stay home one night by ourselves, we open up room for an inward journey to begin. As Twos, we are so naturally wired to find someone to talk to, someone to travel with, someone to pray with, and someone to spend the evening with that we have underdeveloped interior lives. When we reach the end of our ropes and find ourselves needing to shut down for a while, we are invited to discover what's inside. We must face our unknown and repressed longings, feelings, and fears.

But here's the question: Do we have to wait until we have reached the end of our energy to take this inward journey and spend time alone? How much richer could time with ourselves be if we prioritized it and planned for it? Rather than crashing into it, we can intentionally schedule opportunities to be alone and confront the angels and demons inside. If we do, it will pay off in a deeper, more integrated self.

The bad news when we reach these seasons of life is that we are confronted with the reality that we have seen relationships as things to be managed rather than enjoyed. As Twos, we can look at relationships in transactional ways. This is how relationships can sometimes play out for me: *I want to be loved, but I'm not sure that I'm worthy of love, so I settle for being needed. In order to be needed by someone, I look for someone I can help.* The tricky thing is that when I'm tired, I feel like I don't have the capacity to help all these friends anymore, which makes me retreat into a hole of my own making. But what if the invitation in these friendships is for robust enjoyment, not a constant cycle of managed withdrawals and deposits? If I looked at my relationships as being built on foundations of love and mutual enjoyment rather than foundations of expectations, I could save myself some exhaustion!

Jesus offers this parable about the things that last:

> Everyone then who hears these words of mine and acts on them will be like a wise man who built his house on rock. The rain fell, the floods came, and the winds blew and beat on that house, but it did not fall, because it had been founded on rock. And everyone who hears these words of mine and does not act on them will be like a foolish man who built his house on sand. The rain fell, and the floods came, and the winds blew and beat against that house, and it fell— and great was its fall! (Matthew 7:24-27 NRSV)

I am finding my way to becoming the wise man with his house built on the rock by making sure that I am not investing my best foundation stones into relationships built on shifting sand where I play the role of the attentive responder. Instead, I am learning to give my best to relationships that make room for me to be me—holding space for me to just be Hunter, and not have to be Hunter, the happy helper.

> **As you think about your own relationships, how do you see the foundations holding up?**

AVOIDING BURNOUT

ONE OF THE HARDEST PARTS of pastoring for me was dealing with the financial side of church work. Churches need money and pastors have to ask for it, but mixing fundraising with spiritual development is tricky. Books are written and conferences are filled with tips for how to talk to congregations about the gift of giving, but the truth is that it's exhausting for most pastors. Most pastors choose ministry because they want to teach, counsel, and lead, but few are especially gifted with financial management or capital campaigns. The last ten days of December, when a sizeable percentage of our church's annual revenue arrives, were the most hectic and stressful days of the whole year— Merry Christmas!

For the first several years of pastoring, I ended the year feeling burned out and worn out. I assumed that this was because I had worked so hard and given so much, until I read Parker Palmer's *Let Your Life Speak*, a book that has transformed my life. Palmer discusses burnout as something that comes from giving too *little*, not too *much*. According to Palmer, burnout occurs when we give something that we never had to give in the first place. We burn out from trying to give something that isn't within our giftings to give.

I have learned in recent years that the signals of burnout are indicators that I am operating outside of my lane, trying to do something or give something that I don't have. As Twos, most of us have had seasons of life when we have felt the effects of burnout from giving too much in our jobs, our communities, or our relationships. And if you're like me, you probably assume that burnout is the natural result of giving too much.

But what if Palmer is right, and burnout comes from giving too little? What if burnout is the symptom of misplaced efforts on our end? Can we begin to recognize burnout as a clue that we are giving things that were never ours to give?

Twos are givers. But we need to learn how to steward our giving, ensuring that we are spending it in the right places. We need to learn to recognize energy drain, wearing down, and burnout as signals of giving out of scarcity, not abundance.

God of abundance, help me to recognize where you are inviting me to direct my gifts. Fill me with wisdom, guided by the Holy Spirit, to trust the cues of burnout from my body and heart as signals that I have missed your invitation to stop, slow down, and rediscover the things that are truly mine to do. Amen.

MINISTERS OF RECONCILIATION

JESUS IS A RECONCILER of people. The ultimate community builder, Jesus traveled person-by-person after his resurrection to his disciples, who had scattered away. He forgave Peter for his denials. He allowed Thomas to explore his doubt. He chased down the men from Emmaus who left Jerusalem disheartened after seeing their hopes and dreams nailed to a cross. As Christians, we have hope in the ongoing reconciling work of Jesus as he continues to build his kingdom on earth as it is in heaven.

Twos are gatherers of people and reconcilers of those who have wandered away. These are ways that we, in our personalities, carry out the character of Jesus. As we are challenged through this devotional to confront aspects of our personalities that need attention and work, we are also invited to celebrate the unique ways that we, as Twos, join Jesus in his work of community building.

If you are my friend and we experience conflict between us, I'm coming to get you. My friend Vicky, an Enneagram

One with a big Two wing, says, "If I have ever loved you, I still love you." Recently, I had a friendship that felt strained. I wasn't sure exactly what the source was of our misunderstanding, but one thing I knew was that I had to make things right. I went to my friend and asked how we could get back to loving each other well. There is an intuitive orientation to forgiveness and reconciliation that Twos carry—this is our gift to ourselves and our gift to the world.

I love that in Jesus' life on earth, he didn't leave us a book, a list of rules, or a boxed set of recorded teachings. Instead, Jesus left us a meal—a meal to which everyone is invited. Even those of us who are capable of betrayal, like Judas, are invited to the meal. As Twos, we can embrace our gift of setting a place at the table for everyone. This is some of what the world needs from us in a time of polarizing division and scattered relationships.

Reconcilers. Includers. Table-setters. Gatherers. These are names that we should be proud of. They are names that reflect the nature of Jesus himself. It is so important for us to use the Enneagram's wisdom to become the healthiest versions of ourselves so that we can shine our great light to the world: a light that includes, a light that forgives, a light that loves, a light that gathers, and a light that reconciles.

Let's celebrate our light.

> *Reconciling One, show me how I can join you in your work of putting all things back together, on earth as it is in heaven. Amen.*

ACKNOWLEDGMENTS

At the close of this book, I would like to offer the following prayers of gratitude to all—not just those mentioned below—who have set the table for me to share this book with you.

For Suzanne, thanksgivings for introducing and apprenticing me in Enneagram wisdom, spiritual exploration, and abiding lifelong friendship.

For Bradley, thanksgivings for being my cheerleader and awakener.

For my family of origin, Dad, Mom, Holden, Campbell, and Belle, thanksgivings for the thirty-five years of love and lessons to help me discover the man that I am.

For Cindy, thanksgivings for the invitation and opportunity to share my experiences in life and in the Enneagram through these pages.

For my LTM family—Joe, Suzanne, Laura, Joel, Lindsay, Joey, Billy, Carolyn, and Mike—thanksgivings for welcoming me into a community of transformation.

For my LTM Apprentice class, thanksgivings for sharing your lives and wisdom with me for three of the most precious years.

For my first Contemplative Cohort 2019, thanksgivings for offering your heart and soul to Joe and me as we stumbled together toward becoming mystics, falling down and getting back up again.

For the men in my longstanding book and bourbon club—Daniel, Jake, Lewis, Scott, Jay, Tom, Josh, Steven, Mike, Chris—thanksgivings for jumping in on the Enneagram journey with me and celebrating my emerging interest in the early days.

For the early adopters—my first Enneagram companions, who graciously participated in many of my first teachings—I carry you in my heart and in my mind whenever I get the opportunity to teach: Christopher, Amanda P., Stacy, Amanda B., Jessica, Shawne, Tracey, Scott, Jenn, Linda, Ann, Toni, Amanda M., Fran, David, Phil, Abby, Heather, Sharon, Michael, Darin, Colleen, Carmen, Gregg, Brittany, Denise, Daniel, Kristi, Martha, Andy, Diane, Annette, Bob, Brooks, Campbell, and so many others.

And, finally, to the Author, Breather, and Inhabitor of all that is beautiful, true, and good . . . thanksgivings for your unseen hand in bringing me to the gift of the Enneagram and the joy of writing.

NOTES

16 *All healthy religion*: Richard Rohr, "The Sacred Wound," daily email meditation, August 17, 2013.

17 *look away*: "Dixie" is often attributed to minstrel show composer Daniel Decatur Emmett, 1859.

18 *"unconscious" childhood message*: Don Richard Riso and Russ Hudson, *Understanding the Enneagram*, rev. ed. (New York: Houghton Mifflin, 2000), 12.

25 *after the last tear falls*: Andrew Peterson and Andrew Osenga, "After the Last Tear Falls," *Love & Thunder*, Essential, 2003.

29 *The people who plant*: Parker J. Palmer, *Let Your Life Speak: Listening for the Voice of Vocation* (San Francisco: Jossey-Bass, 1999), 32.

32 *If I had to give*: C. S. Lewis, *The Collected Letters of C. S. Lewis, Volume 2, Books, Broadcasts, and the War, 1931-1949*, Walter Hooper, ed. (New York: HarperCollins, 2004), 174.

40 *wounding message*: The wounding messages described here and elsewhere are based on Don Riso's concept of unconscious childhood messages. See Don Richard Riso and Russ Hudson, *Understanding the Enneagram*, rev. ed. (New York: Houghton Mifflin, 2000).

42 *What can be mentioned*: *A Beautiful Day in the Neighborhood*, directed by Marielle Heller (Culver City, CA: Sony Pictures, 2019).

70 *final work, his collected letters*: Henri J. M. Nouwen, *Love, Henri: Letters on the Spiritual Life* (New York: Convergent, 2016).

72 *I began to ask myself*: Henri J. M. Nouwen, *In the Name of Jesus: Reflections on Christian Leadership* (Chestnut Ridge, NY: Crossroad Publishing, 1992), 20.

73 *Twos are thinking-repressed*: Kathleen V. Hurley and Theodore E. Dobson, *What's My Type?* (New York: HarperOne, 1992), 121-30.

97 *Expectations are resentments*: Anne Lamott, Facebook post, November 5, 2014.

105 *Now I have language*: Advanced students of the Enneagram will recognize that the subtypes or instinctual variants play an important role in a person's orientation to community life or isolation, but speaking generally, dependent numbers are often drawn toward community-based expressions of spirituality.

118 *burnout occurs when we give*: Parker Palmer, *Let Your Life Speak: Listening for the Voice of Vocation* (San Francisco: Jossey-Bass, 1999), chapter 3.

ENNEAGRAM
DAILY REFLECTIONS

SUZANNE STABILE,
SERIES EDITOR